Mary and Archie Tisdall have had a life of travel which many would envy. Archie served in the Royal Air Force for forty years and during that time they lived in such diverse countries as Singapore, Jordan, Libya, Tunisia and Malta. Towards retirement they bought a motorcaravan which enabled them to visit further places abroad, principally in Western Europe and gradually they began to write of their experiences for magazines.

They have travelled extensively in Spain, spending many winters in the Canary Islands. This resulted in 1984 in the publication of two guide books, *Tenerife and the Western Canary Islands,* and *Gran Canaria and the Eastern Canary Islands.* Both these books are now in a second impression. Their love of Spain has taken them also to the Balearic Islands, resulting in a further three guide books: *Majorca, Menorca* and *Ibiza & Formentera.* The island series continues in this, their sixth book, about the beautiful Portuguese islands of Madeira and Porto Santo.

They have two sons and two daughters and, when not travelling, live in Salisbury, Wiltshire.

Acknowledgements

The authors would like to thank the following people and organisations for their help, directly or indirectly, in the preparation of this book.
Senhor João Custodia, Director, Portuguese National Tourist Office, London; Senhora Maria Luísa Telo, Secretaria Regional do Turismo e Cultura, Madeira; Senhora Carmelita José Da Gama Melim, Delegação de Turismo, Porto Santo; The Directors, Madeira Sheraton Hotel and Hotel Interatlas, Madeira; Doug Goodman and Julie Torrence, Thomson Holidays Ltd; Simon Spencer, Cosmosair Plc; Senhor Carlos Monteiro, Europeia Agencia Turistica, Funchal; Senhor Ricardo Dias Do Nascimento, Savoy Travel, Funchal; Sharon Alexander, Brittany Ferries; Alan Winn, Sealink, 'Orient Express'.

Our thanks go to Yvonne Messenger, our helpful editor and to our publisher, Roger Lascelles and Bryn Thomas. Finally we acknowledge the interest and encouragement from friends and our family who controls our affairs so well.

Front Cover: *Pico de Arieiro, one of the highest points on the island and the start of a mountain walk.*

Madeira
A Traveller's Guide

Mary and Archie Tisdall

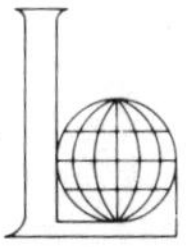

Roger Lascelles, Cartographic and Travel Publisher
47 York Road, Brentford, Middlesex TW8 0QP Telephone: 01-847 0935

Publication Data

Title	Madeira — A Traveller's Guide
Typeface	Phototypeset in Compugraphic Times
Photographs	By the Authors
Printing	Kelso Graphics, Kelso, Scotland.
ISBN	0 903909 77 4
Edition	This First Nov 1989
Publisher	Roger Lascelles 47 York Road, Brentford, Middlesex, TW8 0QP.
Copyright	Mary and Archie Tisdall

All rights reserved. Other than brief extracts for purposes of review no part of this publication may be produced in any form without the written consent of the publisher and copyright owner.

Distribution

Africa:	South Africa —	Faradawn, Box 17161, Hillbrow 2038
Americas:	Canada —	International Travel Maps & Books, P.O. Box 2290, Vancouver BC V6B 3W5
	U.S.A. —	Boerum Hill Books, P.O. Box 286, Times Plaza Station, Brooklyn, NY 1121T, (718-624 4000)
Asia:	India —	English Book Store, 17-L Connaught Circus/P.O. Box 328, New Delhi 110 001
	Singapore —	Graham Brash Pte Ltd., 36-C Prinsep St.
Australasia	Australia —	Rex Publications, 413 Pacific Highway, Artarmon NSW 2064. 428 3566
Europe:	Belgium —	Brussels - Peuples et Continents
	Germany —	Available through major booksellers with good foreign travel sections
	GB/Ireland —	Available through all booksellers with good foreign travel sections.
	Italy —	Libreria dell'Automobile, Milano
	Netherlands —	Nilsson & Lamm BV, Weesp
	Denmark —	Copenhagen - Arnold Busck, G.E.C. Gad, Boghallen, G.E.C. Gad
	Finland —	Helsinki — Akateeminen Kirjakauppa
	Norway —	Oslo - Arne Gimnes/J.G. Tanum
	Sweden —	Stockholm/Esselte, Akademi Bokhandel, Fritzes, Hedengrens. Gothenburg/Gumperts, Esselte. Lund/Gleerupska
	Switzerland —	Basel/Bider: Berne/Atlas; Geneve/Artou; Lausanne/Artou: Zurich/Travel Bookshop

Contents

Appendices

Index

Foreword

This is a guide book for visitors to the beautiful Portuguese archipelago of Madeira, which includes the small sandy island of Porto Santo 46 km to the north east.

Whether you have chosen to go for the peace and quiet, the sunshine, to enjoy the diversity of the countryside and its colourful flora, or just to see somewhere different, this book tells you how to get there, when to go, and what to expect. It describes the different types of accommodation on the islands and gives an idea of local prices. Restaurants, cafés and bars are listed, the costs of car rentals, bus routes and coach excursions are given. You will find notes on the various sports and entertainments that the islands have to offer, and many historic buildings, gardens, churches and museums are described.

Visitors wishing to explore the scenic countryside on foot, by car or coach, will find suggestions for walks and day drives.

There is historical background to the islands too, and local legends and country customs are related so that holidaymakers can gain some understanding of the friendly Madeiran people and their way of life.

We hope your visit to the Madeiran archipelago will be both enjoyable and memorable.

Note: Portuguese is not an easy language to understand or pronounce, but some vocabulary has been given in Appendix A. The map reference and routes used are taken from the *Clyde Leisure Map for the Tourist, No.7. Madeira* ISBN 0-906329-27-2, obtainable from Stanfords Map Centre, 12 Long Acre, London WC2 — £2.75 approx.

All facts and information are as accurate as possible. The currency exchange rate at the time of going to press is 230 escudos to £1, but remember that rates fluctuate and costs increase, so quoted prices should be taken as a guide only.

ONE

Introducing Madeira

The magic of Madeira has been attracting British visitors for more than two hundred years. Centuries before when the first Portuguese explorers discovered the island, they told of a green and enchanted land with a very mild and healthy climate. Since then this tiny subtropical island has been a haven for numerous world weary travellers. Today's tourists benefit from those long forgotten visitors, many of whom added greatly to its charm by introducing different exotic plants and flowers to the already beautiful land. They also brought a tradition of good taste and quiet friendliness that is inherent in the Portuguese and Madeiran way of life.

Nowadays this mountainous island is a blaze of bright coloured flowers, such as the bird-like strelitzia, the anthurium (flamingo flower), the cymbidium (orchid) and the many-hued bougainvillea. Abundant banana plantations mingle with vineyards whose terraces cling perilously to the sides of steep mountain faces. Deep ravines are populated with hard-working farmers growing potatoes and salad crops. Forests of pine and eucalyptus make the air fragrant. Against this panorama of scenic beauty is a dramatic seascape of high cliffs and pounding seas along rocky shores.

Madeira offers the holidaymaker luxurious and comfortable accommodation where the service is friendly and polite. With its interesting cuisine, temperate climate and panoramic scenery, here is an island that is totally different from the usual busy package holiday venue. Yet Madeira is well tuned to receive tourists and strives to provide every facility required. To say that Madeira is a Garden in the Atlantic is no exaggeration and for many it is a floral paradise where they can relax in beautiful surroundings. Mountaineers, hikers and sports enthusiasts all find they can participate in their favourite pastime. Photographers are enraptured at the ever-changing views, where the passing cloud formations, with the high peaks and valleys make a wonderful backcloth for any picture. Artists, too, rush for their colours to record their joy at

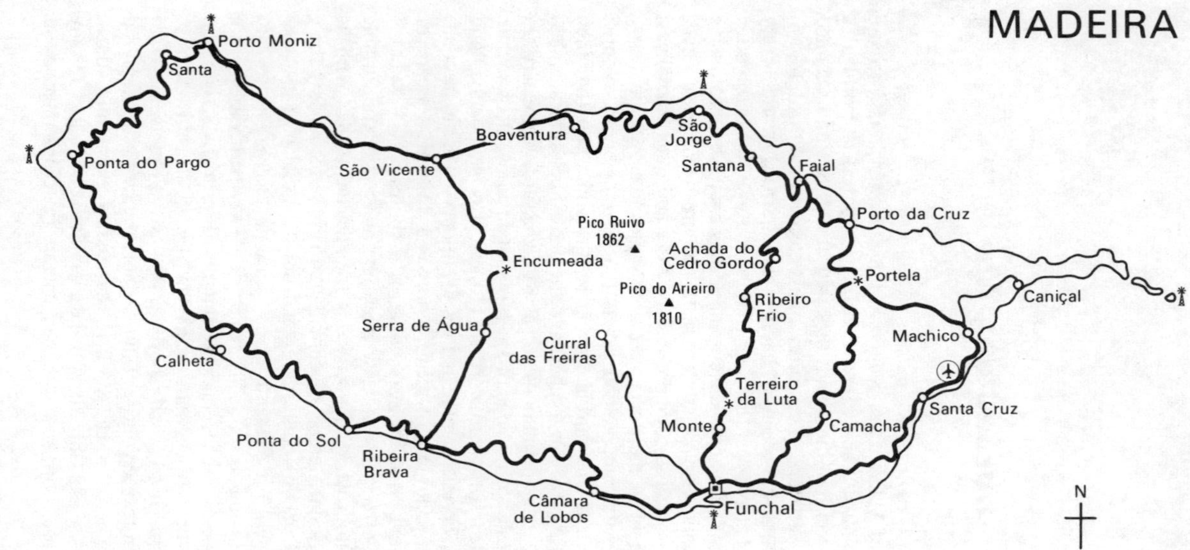
MADEIRA
Porto Moniz
Santa
Ponta do Pargo
São Vicente
Boaventura
São
Jorge
Santana
Faial
Porto da Cruz
Pico Ruivo
1862
Achada do
Cedro Gordo
Encumeada
Pico do Arieiro
1810
Portela
Caniçal
Ribeiro
Frio
Serra de Água
Curral
das Freiras
Machico
Calheta
Terreiro
da Luta
Santa Cruz
Monte
Camacha
Ponta do Sol
Ribeira
Brava
Câmara
de Lobos
Funchal
N
Scale 1:380 000
0
10
20 km

seeing some picturesque fishing village. Madeira is proud of the fact that Sir Winston Churchill delighted in painting at Camâra de Lobos. Lovers of craft and needlework can still see the patient island needle-women at work making delicate lace. The wicker workers of Camacha provide tourists with a lasting and inexpensive souvenir of their stay. You can take something as large as a laundry basket home in the hold of the aircraft!

Botanical experts will delight in the varied gardens of Madeira, especially those of the elegant *quintas,* that pretty Portuguese name for a gracious house with garden and farmlands, where birds and butterflies add to the peaceful scene. Today in Madeira there are no reptiles other than frogs, lizards and various non-poisonous insects.

Apart from all the different pastimes Madeira provides good accommodation which ranges from large five-star luxury hotels in and around Funchal, the capital, to simple *pensoes* (rooms) and *pousadas,* which are country inns. In all these places you will enjoy quiet and efficient service: in Madeira an air of old-fashioned politeness still prevails. Added to all this is a temperate climate which is particularly pleasant for anyone who does not like extremes of cold or heat. Here is a venue where you can take life easily, relaxing in the clean fresh air and sunshine without the hustle and bustle of a noisy background. The fact that Madeira has no beach with any sand, and only a few with pebbles, makes this island different from the usual tourist resorts. Hotels, apartments, clubs and municipalities have pleasant swimming pools with sunbathing areas, suitable for all age groups.

No description of Madeira would be complete without a mention of its *levadas.* In the beginning the *levadas* were built by the farmers who were short of water for their agriculture. A way had to be found to bring water from the mountains and rivers into the centre of the island and to the drier south. So chains of narrow water courses were built to wind their way across the countryside. To walk beside and along these *levadas* is a wonderful way to get to know the interior of Madeira.

Madeiran wine has been a famous Royal favourite for centuries. It is a fortified blended wine made from four principal grape vines grown on the island. Malmsey is the best known: essentially it is a dessert wine for those with a sweet palate. Every visitor is expected to visit a wine lodge in Funchal to enjoy a free taste of the local wines.

Sometimes forgotten is Porto Santo, Madeira's tiny offshore island which lies to the north, a one-and-a-half hour sea crossing from Funchal. Just 41 square kilometres, it is where the people of Madeira go on holiday. The great attraction of Porto Santo is the marvellous sandy beach which runs along the south coast for nine kilometres; this is where sunlovers can get both sea bathing and a glorious suntan. It is almost a desert island; the only nightlife to be found is in the hotels, which are few. Because Porto Santo is flat it boasts a fine runway and many visitors take advantage of the short flight time of twenty-five minutes from Funchal for a full day excursion.

Situation

Madeira is an archipelago in the Atlantic some 500km west of Africa and 978km from Lisbon, consisting of Madeira (population 300,000), Porto Santo (population 5,000), the Ilhas Desertas (desert islands) and the Selvagens (uninhabited). The geographical situation is latitude 32° 38′ N, longitude 16° 54′ W. Tenerife in the Canary islands is 443kms south east and Cape Djouchi in Africa is 545kms away.

Madeira is 57kms long and 22kms wide, a surface area of 740 square kms. Porto Santo, 40 kms north east of Madeira, is only 11kms long and 6kms wide, an area of 41 square kms. Madeira is mountainous, lush and verdant with a rocky coast, whereas Porto Santo is mostly flat with nine kms of golden sandy beach. The Ilhas Desertas, three islands 20km south-east of Funchal, are Ilhéu Chão, Deserta Grande and Bugio. They are all uninhabited, except for some wild goats, rabbits and birds. The Desertas are designated as bird sanctuaries. The Selvagens, 250kms south-east of Madeira, total less than three square kms and are actually nearer to the Canary Islands than Madeira. They are sometimes called 'the Savage Islands', because of their dangerous rocks and barriers. All the islands are of volcanic origin.

The majority of Madeira is a series of high peaks and deep ravines, except for the high and remote plateau of Paúl da Serra, 17kms long and 6kms wide, which rises to 1,500m. The highest point of Madeira is Pico Ruivo at 1,861m. Because of the difficult terrain, cultivating the land has been arduous and farmers have had to build up terraces supported by rock walls. Irrigation is done by using a series of open water drains known as *levadas*.

Manure from the livestock which is kept in sheds, is spread over the terraces and with the mild climate and volcanic soil crops grow quickly. Since it was first discovered Madeira has been on the route to the West Indies and Africa, so becoming an important trading port. Christopher Columbus made three visits to the archipelago and married Isabella Moniz de Perestrelo, daughter of the Governor of Porto Santo (see History Chapter 8). With the advent of commerce the fame of this beautiful island with its mild climate spread to Europe, so in time came rich invalids for convalescence. Finally tourism has assumed a dominant role. With its reputation for peace and quiet amongst gentle people, Madeira is now high on the list of popular destinations.

Climate

Being a small island Madeira is subject to great climatic changes in a short period of time. The winds come mainly from the northeast; the island enjoys a pleasantly mild climate, having the benefit of the Gulf Stream and, in summer, the cool effects of the Trade Winds. With an average temperature of 16°C in January and 21°C in August and a moderate rainfall that is a little higher than the Canary Islands, sea mists and low cloud at higher levels ensure the greenness of the island.

Madeira: average temperatures, air and sea

	Jan	Feb	Mar	Apr	May	Jun	Jul	Aug	Sep	Oct	Nov	Dec
Air °C	16	15	16	17	18	19	20	21	22	22	20	18
°F	62	61	62	63	64	66	68	70	72	72	68	64
Sea °C	17	17	17	18	19	20	21	21	21	20	19	18
°F	63	63	63	64	66	68	70	71	70	68	66	64

Figures published by the Portuguese National Tourist Office, London.

Should the weather by the coast become too bright with sunshine, then an hour's drive into the mountains will refresh you. However, be prepared for swirling mists which can appear suddenly; then, in a few minutes, a fresh breeze will blow the clouds away. Generally the south of Madeira has a milder climate than the north. During

June and July the weather can become humid with heavy clouds. Occasionally a hot dry wind, called a *Leste,* blows across from North Africa: it lasts only a few days. From May to September there is practically no rainfall. In winter, snow or hail can fall on mountain peaks, but probably the sun will be shining in Funchal. Except in the city of Funchal the air is clear, while in the country it is also fragrant with herbs and pine forests. Along the coastline the Atlantic breezes are invigorating. Sea temperatures, influenced by the Gulf Stream, average 22°C in summer and 17°C in winter.

When to go

Madeira is an all the year round destination for holidaymakers. In the past visitors relied mainly on cruise and cargo ships to reach this isolated island. Now, with airports at both Porto Santo and Funchal, tour operators can fly tourists in at all seasons. Described as 'A Floating Garden' Madeira produces floral delights every month, while many flowers bloom the year round.

Generally speaking the high season for accommodation is from December to the end of April, but tariffs vary according to individual hotels and tour companies' itineraries. Because of the mild climate during the winter months the majority of visitors come from the countries in northern Europe, with British tourists topping the numbers list. Summertime sees an influx of Portuguese and Spanish holidaymakers, with Porto Santo being very busy with the Madeirans themselves. Hotels are quiet in the spring and autumn, though this is a time when the countryside is particularly beautiful.

Because of the popularity of Madeira seats on flights can be difficult to get at all times of the year, so it is advisable to make early reservations.

What to pack

You will need a slight variation in clothes depending at which time of the year you intend to visit Madeira, for the temperature can vary some 7°C between winter and summer. For summer days you will require the usual lightweight cottons and drip dry garments, but also take a wrap or cardigan for trips to the mountains. During winter include some thicker garments as the wind can blow cool, especially at night when even a fur coat would not be amiss. All the year you will need sturdy footwear for walking in the mountains and these will be more comfortable, too, on the cobbled streets of Funchal and in some of the villages where there are no pavements.

In general Madeira is not a place to undress, rather the reverse; one sees few bikinis and in town off-the-shoulder dresses do not seem to be correct. To say that Madeira is still old fashioned would be wrong; it is very modern in many ways but with clothes there is still an air of conservatism and graciousness. A degree of formality is expected and observed and this is one of the features that attract many people to this island. The 'way out' clothes that are worn in Ibiza would not look right here. In the higher rated hotels a jacket and tie are requested at dinner and evening dress is not out of place.

Remember to take a sun hat and sun glasses; even in December the sunlight can be strong. Some anti-mosquito cream is essential. Toothpaste, shampoo, cosmetics and other toilet requirements can be purchased locally. Madeira is a delightful place for photographers and most popular makes of films are sold at a slightly higher price than in the UK. Same-day development of films can be done in Funchal.

Binoculars would be a great asset as the views are stupendous, especially along the coastline and in the mountains. If you are on a self-catering holiday you may wish to pack your own special make of teabags, but most groceries and household items are obtainable in supermarkets. Pipe smokers will find that the Portuguese tobacco is similar to Dutch tobacco, cigarette smokers will probably arrive with duty free smokes bought on the aircraft. Popular brands of gin and Scotch whisky are more expensive here than in the UK. English newspapers and paperbacks are on sale but at twice the UK price.

Budgeting for your holiday

The cost of living should not prove higher in Madeira than in Europe or the UK. Generally speaking, package tour holiday-makers require spending money for entertainments, drinks and possibly for additional meals, unless the package includes full board. You must allow for extra costs such as taking part in sports and excursions, the hire of sun umbrellas and chairs, laundry and tips for waiters, maids, porters and taxi drivers. Maybe you will need to buy some extra film for the camera and a few souvenirs and gifts. Prices in tourist areas will probably be a few escudos higher than in Funchal and elsewhere, but if you take into consideration the cost of travelling to a non-tourist place to do your shopping, it will probably work out at much the same.

For the independent traveller or those on a self-catering package it is possible to live quite cheaply by buying local foods. Chickens, eggs, cheese, fruit and vegetables, and some drinks are less expensive than in the UK. Bars and some restaurants are less costly and give good service.

Tourist information

You do not require a visa to stay in Madeira for up to sixty days if you hold a British passport. This period may be extended on application to the Foreigner's Registration Service in Funchal, before the expiry of the initial period. Other passport holders may need a visa, and it is advisable to check with the Portuguese Consulate General, 62 Brompton Road, London SW3. Tel: 01-581 8722. This also applies to those intending to work (or take up work) in Madeira.

You are required to register your arrival and departure in Madeira with the Foreigners' Registration Service in Funchal (Servicio Estrangeiris, Rua da Rochinha). If you are staying in a hotel or residential apartment this will be done for you, but if you are staying privately then you need to make a personal visit to this office within forty-eight hours of arrival and when departing.

Vaccinations are not normally needed for Madeira, only in the case of an epidemic would they be required.

Up-to-date tourist information and leaflets can be obtained from the Portuguese National Tourist Office, New Bond Street House, 1-5 New Bond Street, London W1Y ONP (entrance in Burlington Gardens). Tel: 01-493 3873. The office is open Monday to Friday between 0930 and 1730 hrs. It is closed on public holidays and on 10 June, which is the Portuguese National Day.

Tourist offices in Madeira

The main tourist office in Madeira is the Secretaria Regional do Turismo e Cultura, Avenida Arriaga 18, 9000 Funchal. Tel: 29057. It is open Monday to Saturday from 0900 to 1900 hrs but is closed on public holidays. Other Information Offices are at the Airport, Santa Catarina, Tel: 52933; Edificio Paz, Machico, Tel: 962712; and in Vila Baleiro, Porto Santo, Tel: 982361.

The Portuguese Tourist Office is an official government department with English-speaking staff who will give free information, maps and leaflets. They have a list of hotels and other accommodation and will make reservations for you to stay in the state owned *pousadas* (country inns). They can also supply bus timetables and routes as well as information on special areas of interest such as *levada* walks, shows, concerts, exhibitions and festivals.

Some places of interest

This summary is intended to give you a quick introduction to Madeira and Porto Santo. All the places mentioned here are described more fully in later chapters. Distances from Funchal are shown in brackets.

Funchal

The capital of Madeira and the only city (described in Chapter 9) is in the south of the island. It lies along the waterfront between a wide bay and the hill above, its little narrow steep streets fanning out in a half circle — a fascinating place to explore. Because many of the old roads are still cobbled, sturdy footwear is required and a town plan is useful (obtainable from the Tourist Office).

Camara Municipal The Town Hall is an original eighteenth-century palace with charming patio and facade.

Casa do Turista is a tourist shop, once an old *quinta,* open to the public. A fine display of craft work, ceramics, embroidery and good quality souvenirs is all for sale.

Convento de Santa Clara This fifteenth-century convent and church contains a magnificent Arabic ceiling, beautiful tiles and the tomb of Zarco the explorer.

Fortaleza de São Lourenço The sixteenth century St Lawrence's Fort, a Portuguese national monument, is now the official residence of the Military Governor, with historic cannons and modern soldiers with guns. Not open to the public.

Jardim de São Francisco The Municipal Gardens have a small pond, ducks, fountain and delightful statue. This is a restful place during sightseeing.

Mercado dos Lavradores The Workers Market was built in 1941. Under cover are stalls of vegetables, fruit and colourful flower sellers in national costume. The fish market is downstairs.

Museu de Arte Sacra The Sacred Art Museum, built in 1600 AD, displays religious vestments, sculptures, paintings and church treasures.
Museu Municipal The museum contains marine and natural history collections, also a small aquarium of sea life.
Museu do Vinho da Madeira The Madeira Company Wine Lodge and tasting room is open to the public; you can see a very interesting history of wine-making and old store rooms.
Pálacio do Governo Regional The administrative governmental headquarters is a fine old palace with interesting green shuttered windows and wrought iron gates.
Quinta das Cruzes Set in a magnificent old house, this is a fascinating museum of well-displayed antique furniture, silver, porcelain, paintings and historic treasures. There's an attractive garden with an orchid house and carved stonework. Highly recommended.
Sé Madeira's fine fifteenth-century cathedral is made of volcanic stone and basalt in Manueline Gothic style. The high cedar wood ceiling is inlaid with ivory Mudejar (Moorish) style decor.
Yacht marina and waterfront This is a pleasant place for a stroll to view the cruise ships, fishing boats and pleasure boats. There are kiosk and open air cafés, a garden and seats. The Beatles Boat Restaurant, the rock group's old yacht, is now a tourist feature.

Around Funchal

Jardim Botanico (3km) The Botanical Gardens, in a secluded *quinta* which once belonged to the Reid Family, offer 25,000 square metres of park and gardens, a 'must' for garden lovers. You also have a splendid view of Funchal Bay.
Monte (6kms) This small hillside town is noted for its richly decorated church, Nossa Senhora Do Monte (Our Lady of the Mount), which is the scene of a great pilgrimage on 15 August. Monte is also one of the starting points for the famous Carros de Cesto, the wicker chairs mounted on runners which, like sledges, are toboggan-handled down the steep cobbled streets, carrying squealing tourists to Funchal. Not for the faint-hearted, but most people find this an exhilarating and memorable experience.
Pico dos Barcelos (6kms) Twenty minutes drive from Funchal, this splendid viewpoint overlooking the city and harbour is a stopping place on coach excursions.
Quinta do Palheiro (8kms) Above Funchal are 'Blandy's Gardens', owned by one of the leading families in Madeira. Visits to this

An old fishing boat on one of the golden sandy beaches on the island of Porto Santo, almost a desert island.

extensive tropical garden can be made in the mornings only.
Terreiro da Luta (9kms) This is a viewpoint above Funchal and the first starting place of the toboggan ride down to Monte. The large Monument to Our Lady of Peace was completed in 1927.

North of Funchal

Curral das Freiras (15kms) The Nun's Shelter was so named when the sisters of the Convent in Funchal had to hide away from the pirates in the mountains. A viewpoint overlooks the village.
Faial (33kms) This northern village midst vineyards and sugarcane has a small harbour. Close by is the Penha d'Aguia (Eagle's Rock) where a vast view of the coastline is obtained.
Pico Ruivo (30kms) At 1861m, this is the highest point on the island. It has a Rest House nearby so that climbers can enjoy the famous sunrises and sunsets.
Poiso (20 kms) The starting place for visiting Pico do Arieiro, Poiso, at 1810m is Madeira's second highest peak. A *pousada* and restaurant is being built close to the top. There are amazing views of volcanic mountainsides, sometimes obscured by cloud.
Porto Moniz (98kms) This is a stopping place by the sea for coach excursions. Here great volcanic rocks form pools and tunnels of foaming surf. Bathing is permitted when it is calm. Good restaurants.
Queimadas (63kms) Another high peak (900m), Queimadas has a government rest house and *levada* walks.
Ribeiro Frio (25kms) The name means 'cold stream' and this stream is in a beautiful green valley. There is a Government trout hatchery and botanical gardens. A good place to enjoy an easy *levada* walk.
Santana (39kms) You reach this via Ribeiro Frio. Unique thatched *palheiros* (cottages) are of special interest. There's a large restaurant.

East of Funchal

Camacha (12kms) This is the centre of wickerwork and a flower-growing area. Folklore dances are performed in the restaurant. A starting point for walks.
Canical (33kms) The island's most easterly village has limestone quarries and a small but important fishing port.
Caniço (9kms) This agricultural village is noted for its onions. There is a fifteenth-century chapel.
Machico (26kms) This is where Zarco and Teixeira first landed in 1419. Teixeira's statue stands in front of the fifteenth-century parish

church. There's a wide bay with a harbour and some ship-building. Stony beach.

Ponta de São Lourenço (75kms) This is the most eastern point, with Prainha Bay the only sandy beach on the island. There are interesting rock formations and a lighthouse.

Santa Cruz (20kms) A quiet town with a shingle beach, Santa Cruz has a sixteenth-century church and town hall. It was the second landing place of Zarco, in 1515.

West of Funchal

Câmara de Lobos (9kms) A pretty fishing village set in a small inlet, this is where Winston Churchill painted. You will see why when you look at the gaily coloured fishing boats.

Cape Girâo (19kms) At 550m, this is one of the highest cliffs in the world. A belvedere overlooks the steep drop down to the sea. Warning: if you accept a flower from one of the young children they will expect to be rewarded with escudos!

Encumeada (43kms) The mountain pass set in lush green scenery has views to the north and south.

Estreito de Câmara de Lobos (14kms) This is a famous vine-growing area; the local restaurant specialises in cooking *espetadas,* (meat on skewers).

Paúl da Serra (60kms) This high plateau is in great contrast with the rest of the island. On clear days you can picnic and watch the sheep and goats grazing peacefully. The impressive statue of Senhor de Montanha weighs six tonnes.

Ponta do Sol (50kms) A coastal road with many tunnels and waterfalls leads to this district capital and its rocky beach.

Ribeira Brava (31kms) An important stopping place for tourists visiting the southwestern coast, this seaside town has steep hills either side, a black pebble beach, a few restaurants, and shops.

Porto Santo

Pico do Castelo This volcanic peak is 440m high. A taxi will take you almost to the top where you will be able to view most of the island, including the fine 9km long golden sandy beach and the long airport runway that stretches across the whole width of Porto Santo.

Vila Baleira (also called Porto Santo) The house of Christopher Columbus is here in the tiny capital and is to be restored and made into a museum.

Funchal's harbour provides a safe base for many yachts.

TWO

Getting there

Nowadays Madeira and Porto Santo are accessible by both sea and air, with direct flights from London and Lisbon. Several cargo and cruise ships call at Funchal, especially during the winter months.

By air

The international airport in Madeira, Santa Catarina, was opened in 1964. Since then the runway has been extended and it is planned to lengthen it further out over the bay and part of the Santa Cruz area. This airport is some 22km north east of Funchal, reached by a good fast road most of the way. Only at the outskirts of Funchal is progress slowed by heavy traffic but it is well to remember this when making your own way to the airport.

The airport is an organised and modern building, with a souvenir and duty free shop, travel agent, currency exchange facility, bar, restaurant, car rental and tourist information office. There are luggage trollies, lifts and escalators but no porters. A regular bus service runs between the airport and Funchal (Avenida do Mar).

The airport on Porto Santo has a runway of international standard that is sometimes used for NATO exercises. However, it is mostly used for local services with Madeira. In the rare event of fog or other bad weather at Funchal it is a useful and safe diversion for incoming aircraft. The length of the runway is nearly the width of the island, one end being close to the capital, Vila Baleira, which is also referred to as Porto Santo.

The flight time from London to Madeira is about 3 hours 45 minutes. Scheduled flights are operated direct to Funchal from London Heathrow by TAP Air Portugal. The cost ranges from £186 to £290 return. There are also services via Lisbon. Air Gibraltar operate scheduled flights weekly from London Gatwick direct to Funchal on Saturdays, with return flights Funchal to

Gatwick also on Saturdays. Fares vary according to the time of the year from around £200 to £290 return. In addition there are charter flights from Heathrow, Gatwick and Manchester A charter flight costs from £154 to £190 return.

Among the tour operators who offer package holidays to Madeira are Abeu Tours, Cadogan, Caravella Tours (TAP), Cosmos, Enterprise, Hays and Jarvis, HF Holidays (Walking), Suntours, Thomas Cook, Thomson Holidays and Wings. Thomson Holidays have recently commenced Young at Heart Winter Sunshine Holidays, which seem good value for the over fifty-fives.

Inter island flights

There are three return flights daily between Funchal and Porto Santo, operated by TAP Air Portugal (in a DHT Twin Otter Aircraft). The flight takes about twenty-five minutes and costs 4560 escudos (£19.80) return. Reservations can be made at the TAP Air Portugal offices (Avenida Do Mar, Funchal. Tel: 52864) and at travel agents.

Cruise ships approaching Madeira have a good view of the island with its many palm trees.

By sea

A number of cruise ships call at Funchal and, on some, passengers can break their voyage and stay on the island.

Cruise ships arriving at Funchal harbour are met with a wide vista of the fine old city that lies in the centre of a sheltered bay; steep streets full of square white houses lead up the green slopes of the hillside behind the harbour. Red-tiled roofs merge with dark pines and tropical palm trees. A long modern jetty, the Pontinha, allows a berth for several cruise ships at a time, while the cargo and fishing vessels moor along the town side of the harbour. An old fortress, the Nossa Senhora Da Conceição, reminds newly arrived passengers that pirates were once a menace to this now peaceful harbour. The modern yacht marina is well sheltered and very close to the heart of the city. A cargo ship, the *Empresa National Madeirense,* sails once a week between Lisbon and Funchal and will carry a few passengers and cars.

Inter island ferry

A modern catamaran, called the *Indêpendencia,* carries 244 passengers between Funchal harbour and Porto Santo. It makes two return crossings daily in the summer and one in winter. Each way takes about one and a half hours and costs 3,500 escudos (£15.21) return, 2,000 escudos (£8.70) single. The *Indêpendencia* travels at a speed of thirty knots and at times the crossing can be very rough. No meals are served on board. There are stewards on hand to help you but the atmosphere on board is stuffy and slightly claustrophobic.

Private yachts

Funchal has a small yacht marina. It is sheltered by the main harbour and lies close to the city centre on the Avenida Do Mar. Water and electrical points are provided on the pontoons and the use of these is included in the daily charge for mooring. Camping Gaz refill 907 cylinders are available. The marina appears to be well patrolled by police.

Daily charges for vessels are by length: 10 metres = 1000 escudos (£4.34); 15 metres = 1500 escudos (£6.52); above 15 metres = 2500 escudos (£10.86). Add 12 per cent tax.

Seen from the beach the Dom Pedro Hotel at Machico looks strikingly modern.

THREE

Where to stay

The hotels in Madeira are of a high standard: more than 32 per cent of the 10,322 beds on the island are in five-star hotels, while a further 20.4 per cent are in four-star properties. At present only 9 per cent are in the three-star category. No two-star or one-star places are listed. The remainder of the accommodation is largely in apartments, guesthouses, *pensoes* (pensions), *pousadas* (inns) or in the Matur Tourist Complex which consists of villas and apartments. *Albergarias* are older style establishments with character providing a room and usually serving breakfast only. Apartment Hotels consist of apartments with private bathroom and kitchenettes, with a minimarket available nearby. Hotels in the de luxe five-star category are of international class situated in excellent locations.

The emphasis on high-class accommodation is a deliberate policy of the Portuguese National Tourist Office and the Government of Madeira; it is felt that if Madeira is to preserve its environment and standards there is just not enough space on the island to accommodate a mass tourist market.

The construction of three more four-star hotels in Funchal has begun and the five-star Sheraton Hotel will be opening a further 102 rooms in time for the winter season 1988/89.

The star rating

Accommodation in Madeira is officially put into three groups: hotels, hotel apartments, and others. Prices, daily, for a double room, in these groups are:

Group 1

Five-star hotel, from 6,600 to 23,000 escudos.
Four-star hotel, from 4,200 to 16,000 escudos.
Three-star hotel, from 4,000 to 9,200 escudos.

Group 2
Four-star hotel apartment, from 4,000 to 9,200 escudos.
Three-star hotel apartment, from 3,600 to 9,000 escudos.
Two-star hotel apartment, from 3,500 to 5,000 escudos.

Group 3
Four-star pension, from 2,900 to 5,200 escudos.
Three-star pension, from 2,500 to 5,200 escudos.
Two-star pension, from 2,500 to 3,000 escudos.

There are also *pousadas* (country inns), which range in price from 3,700 to 4,900 escudos per day.

Children under the age of eight are entitled to a discount of 50 per cent if they share a room with their parents. Cots can be provided if the hotel is notified at the time of booking.

A selection of accommodation in Madeira and Porto Santo is given below, listed alphabetically under group and star rating. Prices quoted are for accommodation arranged privately, not package holiday costs.

A selection of accommodation in Madeira

Group 1: hotels

Atlantis (five-star) Água de Pena, Machico. Tel: 962811. 300 rooms and 18 suites all airconditioned, with radio and terrace. Situated on the south east coast of Madeira this modern luxury hotel is fifteen minutes from the airport and ten minutes from the little town of Machico. The hotel has a relaxed atmosphere and offers an indoor swimming pool, nightclub and a full entertainment programme. Amenities include an à la carte restaurant, spacious lounge, TV room, table tennis, mini golf and archery. Sauna, hairdresser, shopping centre, playground, babysitting service and early suppers for children. The Atlantis is part of the self-contained Matur Holiday Village, which itself offers an Olympic size pool, disco, night club, three restaurants and three bars.

Casino Park (five-star) Avenida do Infante, Funchal. Tel: 33111. 400 rooms, 20 suites and 32 studios, all airconditioned with private bathroom, balcony and sea view. The hotel was designed by Oscar Niemeyer, principal architect of Brazil's new capital city Brasilia. The overall scene is very modern and matches the adjoining Casino.

The dining room and grill room offer international cuisine. The swimming pool overlooks Funchal harbour. Many amenities include a children's play area, tennis, billiards, hairdresser, shopping arcade, beauty salon, health centre with jacuzzi and a steam bath. There's a conference room.

Palácio (five-star) Estrada Monumental, Funchal. Tel: 30001. 260 rooms, 18 suites all with bathroom and spacious balcony. Rooms also have TV and video. This modern well-appointed hotel is some five kilometres westwards from Funchal and well away from the tourist area. It offers a variety of dining rooms: the Cristavoa Colombo room specialises in local sea foods: the Vicerei Grill in grills and roasts; there's also the Terrace Café, the Gazebo Bar and the Chin Chin bar by the pool. Dicoteca 145 opens every evening, and every week there's a folklore group. Amenities are heated swimming pool, two tennis courts, badminton, sauna, hairdresser, bridge room, games and children's room. There are conference facilities for 300.

Reid's Hotel (five-star) Estrada Monumental, Funchal. Tel: 23001. Open all year. 165 rooms and 15 suites. One of the world's most famous hotels, this was built by William Reid and opened in 1891. The founder had arrived from Scotland at the age of fourteen with only £5 in his pocket. He first worked in a bakery then took to letting *quintas* (large houses) on behalf of Madeiran and foreign owners. Later he turned one of these *quintas* into a hotel and eventually bought the land to build his luxury dream hotel, Reid's Palace Hotel; but sadly he died in 1888, aged sixty five, before the hotel was finished. In 1925 the Reid brothers (William Reid's sons) sold the hotel to an English company and in 1937 it was again sold to the present owners, the Blandy family (Island Hotel Madeira Ltd), but it has always been known as Reid's Hotel. Today the hotel is well known for its old style of quiet luxury and fine position on a headland overlooking Funchal. Most of its clients are elderly rich people, who enjoy the good service, peace and beauty of the ten acres of fine exotic gardens. Reid's culinary expertise extends to serving afternoon tea with much decorum and elegance (1,100 escudos £5 per person). There are two restaurants and a grill room, two airconditioned cocktail bars, two heated swimming pools, and a jetty for seabathing and sunbathing terrace. Other amenities are dancing every night, a health centre, sauna, hairdresser and beauty salon.

Savoy (five-star) Avenida do Infante, Funchal. Tel: 22031. 347 rooms with bathroom and balcony, and 12 suites. This luxurious hotel has an air of elegance, a tranquil atmosphere and is beautifully furnished with deep carpets, oil paintings and marble columns in the public rooms. Sub-tropical gardens lead to a private shopping arcade and aquatic sports. The view is over Funchal Bay. It is a fifteen-minute walk downhill to the city centre. The hotel has restaurant and grill room, two bars (one has dancing nightly), the Galaxia Nightclub, two heated swimming pools, sun terraces and a jetty for sea bathing. There are two tennis courts, hairdresser, sauna, gymnasium, games room and mini golf. Conference facilities are available.

Sheraton (five-star) Largo Antonio Nobre, Funchal. Tel: 31031. Telex 72122 Sherfu P. 292 rooms, 15 suites. Opened in 1971, the Madeira Sheraton is built on the side of a cliff with the large reception area on the sixth floor. Visitors will immediately be impressed with the quiet and efficient manner of the staff and the tasteful decor of the hotel, especially the attractive and spectacular floral displays. Fully air conditioned guestrooms and suites have private bathrooms. All have private balconies or terraces with fine views, radio, telephone and room service. The restaurant has an elegant decor and extensive sea view. Breakfast is 'help yourself', with waiter service. Portuguese specialities are served in the intimate and candlelit O Churrasco Grill. Marinated raw fish is 950 escudos (£4.13), grilled lamb cutlets 2,950 escudos (£12.82), and desserts from the trolley 650 escudos (£2.82). Lunch can be taken by the heated swimming pool on the terrace where there is also a children's swimming pool. Especially pleasant is afternoon tea, served from 1600 to 1800 hrs; tea and cakes for two costs 500 escudos (£2.17). The Taverna Bar has live music every evening. Whisky costs 380 escudos (£1.65) and a local beer 250 escudos (£1.12).

In the grounds are gardens and layout chairs for sun-bathing. A second swimming pool is at a lower level close to the Atlantic ocean: you can also swim in the sea from the rocks. Other amenities are tennis courts, mini golf, table tennis, billiards, health club with sauna, hairdresser and shops. The hotel is a ten-minute walk downhill into the centre of Funchal. There is a bus service into town and a bus stop is just outside the hotel. The high season tariff is charged 22 December — 5 January, and from 27 March — 6 April; low season tariff for the rest of the year. Prices (1988) per night for two persons, bed and breakfast depend on type of accommodation

You can be sure of a comfortable hotel in Madeira.

as well as seasonal tariff: standard mountain view, high 21,000 escudos (£91.30), low 14,000 escudos (£60.86); superior seaview, high 25,000 escudos (£108.70), low 18,500 escudos (£80.44); cliff and standard suite, high 31,500 escudos (£137), low 24,500 escudos (£106.52). Half board per person daily, 3,100 escudos (£13.47); full board per person daily, 5,200 escudos (£22.60).

Dom Pedro (four-star) Machico. Tel: 962751. 28 rooms with seaview, bathroom and heating. Close to the wide bay of Machico and five minutes drive from the airport, this is a family hotel with a relaxed atmosphere. The entertainments programme includes folklore, fado and dancing. Amenities include a heated sea water pool and paddling pool, tennis courts and volley ball, an international windsurfing school, big game fishing excursions. A bus service runs between Machico and Funchal 24 kilometres (15 miles) to the southwest.

Girassol (four-star) Estrada Monumental, Funchal, tel: 31051. 136 rooms all with private baths and seaview. This is an established hotel on the outskirts of Funchal, ten minutes by bus to the centre, to which many British tourists return each year. The restaurant has international menus, bar, dancing and night club. A terrace on the twelfth floor has panoramic views. Amenities are heated swimming pool, sports facilities and shopping centre nearby.

Quinta Do Sol (four-star) Rua Do Pinta 6, Funchal. Tel: 31151. 118 rooms and 7 suites with bathroom, balcony and airconditioning. The hotel is in a lovely green setting up a slight hill, about two kilometres from the centre of Funchal. The rooftop terrace has a magnificent view over the city. It is about a ten-minute walk downhill to the nearest bars and restaurants. There's a heated swimming pool and a children's pool, and early suppers are provided. Next door is the Country Club with tennis courts and an eighteen-hole putting green.

São João (four-star) Rua das Maravilhas, Funchal. Tel: 46111. 192 rooms and 16 suites, all with bathroom and terrace, air conditioning and music. Situated on a hillside in the residential area of Funchal (it could be difficult for the physically handicapped), this is a comfortable and friendly hotel. There are three restaurants that serve typical local food. A very steep walk leads downhill to a stony beach with a small bar. The night club has live music, singing and talent competitions. Amenities are a covered swimming pool, physical fitness classes and games room. There is a hotel bus into

Funchal. Coach excursions can be booked and cars rented at the hotel. A double room with breakfast per night costs 6,600 escudos (£28.69).

Vila Ramos (four-star) Azinhaga da Casa Branca 7, Funchal. Tel: 31181. 104 rooms with bathroom and balcony. This hotel is about three kilometres from the centre of the city, in a hillside area amid banana plantations. It's a friendly place for those who like a quiet venue away from the seafront. It has an outdoor heated swimming pool and sun terraces, tennis courts, billiards, TV and card rooms.

Santa Isabel (three-star) Avenida do Infante, Funchal. Tel: 231115. 59 rooms and 10 suites all with bathroom and balcony. This is a small hotel situated next door to the Savoy Hotel, on the main road which leads two kilometres downhill to the centre of Funchal. An attraction for guests is the use of the prestigious facilities of the Savoy and free entry to the night club. Early suppers for children and cots are available.

Group 2: hotel apartments

Inter Atlas (three-star) Garaju, Caniço. Tel: 932421. 126 apartments each with bathroom, kitchenette, balcony and seaview. This is a friendly place situated in quiet countryside and with helpful staff, but in need of renovation at time of writing. It has two swimming pools, one indoor and heated, the other outdoor and ten minutes walk downhill. There is a useful supermarket, a small souvenir shop, TV room, two bars and some evening entertainment. There is no courtesy bus but the local bus goes to Funchal five times a day. The cost of a taxi to Funchal is 800 escudos (£3.47). Caniço, the nearest village is a thirty-five minute walk along a road without pavements.

Group 3: other accommodation

Cathedral (four-star *albergaria*) Rua do Aljube 13. Tel: 30091. Funchal. 25 rooms with bath. Conveniently situated close to the Cathedral and the centre of the city. This is a useful and well appointed *albergaria* for anyone who requires just a clean, comfortable room with a private balcony. A small public terrace has a good view of the city, sea and harbour below. The small lounge has a bar and there is a lift. Open all the year, the cost for a double room with breakfast per night is 4,000 escudos (£17.39).

Residencial Monte Rosa (four-star pension) Rua de João Tavira 31, Funchal. 38 rooms with bath and 1 suite. Situated in the centre of the city, above a shopping street. This is a clean and simple, rather old fashioned pension with a roof terrace overlooking the sea. A double room with breakfast per night costs 4000 escudos (£17.39). It is open all the year.

Vinhaticos *(pousada)* Serra de Água. 10 rooms with bath, a restaurant, bar and sitting room. This *pousada* is located just off the road to Encumeada, in a splendid mountain setting 660 metres high. This is an idyllic place for country lovers who wish to walk nearby. A double room with breakfast per night costs 4,400 escudos (£19.30).

A selection of accommodation in Porto Santo

Note that the water from the taps in Porto Santo is not considered suitable for drinking. At times there can be a shortage of water. Supermarkets and bars sell bottled drinking water.

Group 1: hotels

Porto Santo (four-star hotel) Porto Santo 9400. Tel: 982381. 98 rooms with bath and 2 suites. This pleasant two-storey hotel, owned by Trusthouse Forte Hotels, is set very close to the long sandy beach. The green lawns, swimming pool and sunterraces provide a restful venue, an oasis in an almost desert island. Airconditioned public rooms are nicely furnished and everywhere is well maintained. There is a tennis court, windsurfing, and ideal sea bathing. This high class hotel is often fully booked during July and August. A double room with breakfast per night costs 5,865 escudos (£25.50), half board 8,855 escudos (£38.50), full board 11,730 escudos (£51). Charges are a little higher in winter.

Prai Dourada (three-star hotel) Porto Santo 9400. Tel: 982315. 35 rooms with bath and music. A small but nicely appointed modern hotel in the centre of the tiny capital, Vila Baleira. A double room with breakfast per night costs from 4,600 to 7,000 escudos (£20—£30.43).

Group 3: other accommodation

Pensão Central (three-star pension) Rua Abel Magno Vasconelos, Porto Santo. Tel: 982226. 12 rooms with small bathrooms. Clean, pleasant, old fashioned accommodation, with tiny bar and nice sun terrace. Planning permission has been given for modernisation and the addition of more rooms. A double room with breakfast costs per night in summer 3,650 escudos (£15.86), in winter 2,600 escudos (£11.30).

Pensão Palmeira (three-star pension) Porto Santo. Tel: 982112. 23 rooms with small bathroom. Modest, clean accommodation near to the centre of town. A double room with breakfast per night costs 3,500 escudos (£15.21).

Apartments Zarco Rua João Concalves Zarco 66, Porto Santo. Tel: 982273. Tucked away in a side street of Vila Baleira amongst the locals, rooms and simple apartments are being converted for European tourists. Some English is spoken here. A double room with bath per night costs 2,200 escudos (£9.56), with kitchenette, 3,500 escudos (£15.21), and a studio 4,000 escudos (£17.39).

Camping

Madeira has no official camp sites, but on Porto Santo a new camping park has recently been opened.

At Porto Moniz in the north west of Madeira there is a small and simple unofficial camping area close to shops, sea and restaurants. This is suitable for campers who are travelling with a small tent. The village can be reached using the local bus service from Funchal, or by taxi. This is a splendid place for anyone wishing to spend a few days in a remote area close to the Atlantic Ocean, with great towering cliffs, seabirds and a few villagers for company. It is very peaceful here, except when taxis and coaches arrive bringing tourists to the popular and good fish restaurants for lunch. Also this is an especially interesting venue because at the water's edge dark black volcanic rocks lie in weird and fantastic shapes. These form pools of water which, according to weather and tide, can sometimes be perfectly calm and a beautiful translucent aquamarine, or at other times a roar of foaming white spume from the raging seas as the great Atlantic rollers pound the rocks. During the summer months it can be safe enough to bathe in the rock pools and you will have the local Madeirans for company. Camp charges are modest: 100 escudos (£0.43) per person and the same for a tent, per day.

The camping park on Porto Santo is a municipal campsite run by the Região Autónoma da Madeira. Still in the early stages of completion, this camp will eventually be first class and offer very modern facilities. It is situated in the capital, Vila Baleria, and lies right alongside the nine kilometres of wonderful golden sandy beach with a gate from the camp that leads to the sand dunes.

The area of this camp site is completely level and sandy. At present there is no shade as the newly planted trees are still small, so that at midday it could be very hot. However, there are excellent buildings spaced out and designed to provide a rest room, games room and reading room. Here, too, are modern toilet blocks, laundry, cooking and washing up facilities. A large supermarket is so well stocked that the local residents use it for their daily shopping. A bar and restaurant are under construction.

For many this is ideal camping in Porto Santo.

There is a resident warden and the camping regulations extend to four pages on the subject of admission and registration. The camp site is designed for long or short stays for tents, caravans and motorcaravans. Campers must produce an International Camping Carnet or their passport. Anyone under the age of fifteen must be accompanied by an adult. Tents need to be pitched at least two metres apart. The local authorities are keen to make this an orderly camp so they have issued twenty-four rules of discipline. The camp is open all the year. Charges per day are: adults over 25 years 100 escudos (£0.43), under 25 years 50 escudos (£0.22), children under 5 years free; small tent 100 escudos (£0.43), large tent 150 escudos (£0.65).

Package holidays

There are several UK companies that operate package holidays to Madeira. They offer holidays throughout the year and generally provide very good value for money. By booking this type of holiday it allows you to budget in advance for most of your expenses.

When you book a package the cost includes accommodation, air fare and transport between where you are staying in Madeira and the airport. Tour operators' brochures, obtained from UK travel agents, give details of flight arrangements, type of resort, star rating of hotel or apartment, meal arrangements and what you can expect in the way of entertainments and sport.

On arrival at the airport in Madeira you will be met by the tour company representative. He or she will assist you to a coach which will then take you to your accommodation. This courier will meet you again for a welcoming party and you will be informed of local interests, excursions and entertainments. It is recommended that you use the services of your courier, who has up-to-date information on the locality and about good eating places. These representatives are generally helpful, hard working and patient.

Some of the holiday firms offer two-centre package deals with one week on sandy Porto Santo and another in Madeira. Thomson Holidays, who claim to have forty per cent of the market, include a Young at Heart brochure which caters for those who expect entertainment at their hotel. It has been said that people who go to Madeira seem to prefer the higher star rated hotels. The trend also seems to be for bed and breakfast only, owing to the increase in the number of restaurants in Madeira.

HF Holidays in conjunction with TAP Air Portugal, have special holidays designed for the walker. Making use of the local bus service, the couriers take their guests to starting points for guided walks which explore the *levadas,* along rugged sea cliffs, and to the high peaks of the island.

Taking the children

The Madeirans are fond of children but expect them to be quiet and well behaved; rarely do you see their children tearing about and making a nuisance. The hotels and apartments provide cots, high chairs and early suppers. Dried milk, disposable nappies and baby foods are available in chemists and some supermarkets. Imported brands are a little more expensive than in the UK.

This is an island that does not provide a lot of entertainment specially for children. The larger hotels have separate paddling pools for youngsters. For older children there is swimming, tennis, table tennis, crazy golf, windsurfing and plenty of walking. The Municipal Museum in Funchal has a small aquarium with live underwater creatures, and the Firemen's Museum should provide interest. Some hotels show films and videos and have their own discos and floorshows. Folk dancing groups can be seen in restaurants and hotels.

When going on coach excursions with young children remember that toilet facilities are not frequent, and because the country roads are narrow it is difficult for coaches to make 'comfort' stops; so when the coach does make a stop it is wise to take advantage of the toilet facilities of the nearest café.

Taking pets

If you wish to take your cat or dog with you to Madeira you will require a health and Rabies Inoculation Certificate (enquire at the Portuguese National Tourist Office, New Bond Street House, 1/5 New Bond Street, London W1Y ONP. Tel: 01 493 3873). Remember, however, that on your return to the UK your pet will have to spend six months in quarantine.

The Society for the Protection of Domestic Animals, Rua do Matadouro, Funchal, Tel: 20852, has a small veterinary clinic. It is open Monday to Friday 1530 to 1930 hrs and on Saturday from 1000 to 1200 hrs.

Travel agents

There are numerous travel agents in Funchal, in the Lido area to the west and the resorts of Água de Pena (Matur) and Porto Santo. Their services vary; they may be agents for hotels, apartments, ferries, cruises, flight reservations, self-drive car rental, coach excursions and currency exchange. Many of the staff speak English. Their offices are open from 0900 to 1230 and from 1430 to 1800 hrs, Monday to Friday, and some open on Saturday mornings. Amongst the travel agents in Funchal are:

— **Abreu** Avenida do Infante 22. Tel: 31077
— **Blandy Brothers** Avenida de Zarco 14. Tel: 20161
— **Euromar** Avenida do Infante 59. Tel: 20152
— **Melia** Avenida de Zarco 14. Tel: 33435
— **Savoy Travel** Avenida do Infante. Tel: 31151
— **Star Travel** Avenida Ariaga 23. Tel: 32001 (levada walks)
— **Viva Travel** Rua Serpa Pinto 32. Tel: 31064

Outside Funchal are:

— **Rota do Atlantico** Agua de Pena, (Matur). Tel: 962725
— **AB Tours** Rua João Gonçalves Zarco, Porto Santo. Tel: 982175
— **Blandy Brothers** Avenida Dr Manuel Pestana Júnior, Porto Santo. Tel. 982114

Property and estate agents

Madeira presents an appealing location for purchasers to invest in property. Many British people have owned property there for a long time and are accepted into the local community. It is advisable to get specialist advice on the subject because the Portuguese method of property transaction differs from that in the UK.

The selling of apartments and villas, the administration of property, letting, legal advice, repairs, technical services and insurance is carried out by real estate companies in Madeira. Some have connections with the UK, and many of the firms employ

English-speaking staff trained to assist clients. Some estate agents in Madeira are:

— São Goncalo Estate, Estrada Monumenta 189, Funchal. Tel: 25085
— Aniball de C.Talhadas, Centro Comercia Infante, Loja 218, 9000 Funchal. Tel: 20880/29219
— Estate Agents Efebe, Rua 31 de Janeiro 85A. Tel: 33351/22722
— Alvaro Nunes, Largo do Chafariz 16-2. Tel: 21393
— Centromar, Pinta da Cruz, São Martinho. Tel: 20430
— Unicon Lda (also a law service agency) Sala 312, Andar Edificio a Torre, Rua dos Murcas 42, 9000 Funchal. Tel: 25455/00603/27395

Time share

The Madeira Beach Club, in association with Madeira Sheraton Hotels, offer weekly ownership of apartment suites with full room service, laundry, dry cleaning, porter service and doctor on call for twenty-four hours, The Madeira Beach Club is fully integrated with the Madeira Sheraton Hotel. For details, Madeira Beach Club, PO Box 1, Funchal 9000, Madeira. Tel: 23521.

FOUR

Getting about Madeira

There are no trains in Madeira. The old funicular railway from Funchal to Terreiro da Luta ceased to operate some forty-five years ago but part of this route can still be travelled down hill on the famous wooden toboggans. (See page 129).

Some main roads in Madeira are good though there are no motorways. However, in the country most of the roads are narrow with a poor, sometimes cobbled, surface. Mountain approaches can be steep with many hairpin bends and blind corners making driving slow and tiring.

Walking is a very popular and satisfactory way of seeing the country and mountains. Using the *levadas* and footpaths is an invigorating pastime. A good road and footpath map of Madeira is essential if you want to get about and see the island. Recommended is Clyde Leisure Map No.7 Madeira (ISBN 0-906329-27-2) in the series published by Clyde Surveys Ltd, Reform Road, Maidenhead, Berks SL6 8BU. Tel: 0628 21371. This map can also be obtained from Stanfords Map Centre, 12 Long Acre, London WC2. Price £2.75. A most useful and detailed book for walkers is *Landscapes of Madeira* by John and Pat Underwood (see Bibliography).

Driving in Madeira

It is unlikely that you will ship your vehicle to Madeira for a short stay holiday as this would be a tedious and expensive undertaking. However, you may wish to rent a self-drive car. Remember that there are only a few petrol stations outside of Funchal, so it is best always to set off with a full tank, because steep climbs and slow driving on narrow roads will consume more fuel. At the time of writing the cost of Super petrol is 105 escudos (£0.46) a litre, Normal (2-star) 101 escudos (£0.44), and Diesel 63 escudos (£0.27).

In Madeira driving is on the right-hand side of the road. It is the rule to give way to traffic coming from the right unless otherwise indicated. The wearing of seat belts is compulsory and non-wearers can be fined. Despite this, you will notice a number of Madeiran drivers not using their seat belts. It is illegal to park on the side of the road facing oncoming traffic. In Funchal, there are carparks and parking meters but never enough for the number of vehicles there. The speed limit in town is 60 kph (37.5 mph) and elsewhere on the island 90 kph (56 mph), but in the country it is not possible to reach anything like that speed because of the mountainous terrain and slow country traffic. It is advisable to be alert to sudden hazards like potholes, falls of rock, and animals, and certainly at some time you will go through mist, even cloud. Do not be reluctant to sound your horn; this is essential when overtaking. In towns there are traffic lights and pedestrian crossings.

Road signs

International road signs are used in Madeira. In addition, some notices are written in Portuguese. It is a good idea to memorise the translation of the more important ones:

Alto	Halt
Encruzilhada/Cruzamento	Crossroads
Perigo/Perigosa	Danger
Descida ingreme	Steep hill
Desvio	Diversion
Paragem	Bus stop
Pare	Stop
Passagem prohíbida/ Sentido prohíbida	No entry
Sem saida	No through road

Tourist attractions and some restaurants have large blue and yellow signposts

Self drive car hire

For those who desire to discover the panoramic delights of Madeira on their own, the car hire firms are numerous. (Some with international names will also provide drivers if required.) It is advisable to book your vehicle a few days in advance to avoid disappointment. Unlimited mileage is included in the cost, but not fuel. A tax of 12 per cent and vehicle insurance are added. Personal accident insurance is optional but advisable: to cover the driver and all passengers costs about 200 escudos (£0.86) a day.

To hire a car you generally have to be at least 23 years of age with a minimum of one year's driving experience. You will have to produce your driving licence or, better still, an international driving permit which carries your photograph. (Obtainable from AA or RAC.) Sometimes a deposit is requested (or payment in advance) in the region of 5,000 escudos. International credit cards (Visa, Access, etc) are accepted for payment.

Some idea of daily rental charges is given below. There is a slight reduction for longer periods of hire.

Renault 4 GTL	5300 escudos (£23)
Opel Corsa or Renault 5TL	5600 escudos (£24)
Renault Laureate	6500 escudos (£28)
Peugeot 205 GL	6700 escudos (£29)
Mercedes Benz 230	18000 escudos (£78)

Car rental can be arranged through travel agents, hotel reception desks and at the airport. Some of the firms in Funchal who handle car hire are:

— **Atlas** Rua da Algeria 23. Tel: 23100
— **Avis** Largo António Nobre 164. Tel: 64546
— **Bravacar** Rua da Carreira 52B. Tel: 26444
— **Europcar** Rua Ivens 13-B. Tel: 20542
— **Hertz** Rua Ivens 12. Tel: 25619
— **Rodavante** Rua Nova da Quinta Deão 19. Tel: 47448.

Taxis

In Funchal there is no shortage of taxis. They are distinctively painted yellow and blue, are clean, and generally give good service. Compared to prices in Europe the fares are quite cheap. If you are the only passenger you are expected to sit in the front with the driver. Taxis in the city of Funchal are required to have meters, but in some cases they do not use them, so it is advisable to agree the price before getting into the vehicle. It costs about £2—£3 for a journey from the city centre to the outskirts. A taxi rank is located by the Cathedral in Funchal. Your hotel reception or hall porter will be able to order you a taxi.

Taxis are used extensively by tourists making island tours. The prices are advertised and are generally in the region of 8000 escudos (£35) for a full day tour and 5000 escudos (£22) for a half day. The fare will be the same however many people are using the taxi. You will be taken to places of notable interest and to viewing points, all with a commentary in English. Stops will be made when you wish, including time for lunch on the day tour. Taxi drivers expect a tip of about 10 per cent.

Some examples of popular taxi tours are shown below. The prices are those quoted by the Madeira Tourist Office in Funchal.

- Funchal, local tour.
  Hotel to Monte, visit to gardens and church, return. 1,900 escudos (£8.26).
- To the east.
  Hotel to Camacha, visit to wicker work factory, return. 3,000 escudos (£13).
  Hotel to Machico, Caniçal, Prainha, Santa Cruz (with stops), return. 4,000 escudos (£17.39).
- To the west
  Hotel to Câmara de Lobos, Pico da Torre, Cabo Girão, Companário, Ribeira Brava, Encumeada, San Vicente, Seixal, Porto Moniz, Santana, Faial, Poiso, Monte, return. 8,000 escudos (£34.38).

Buses

Madeira is well served by buses and this is a pleasant way of travelling. You can obtain a comprehensive timetable from the Tourist Office in Funchal. Buses run to all parts of the island but the more remote places have a less frequent service. It is best to check that you are able to return from your country destination on the same day; it may also be necessary to reserve a seat.

All the buses in Funchal leave from stops (*paragem*) along the seafront known as Avenida do Mar (Avenida do Mar e das Comunidades Madeirenses). There are ticket offices for some of the routes, otherwise you pay on entry, or wait until a conductor collects your fare. Orange buses travel to points within the city and an average fare is about 115 escudos (£0.50). It should be noted that buses within Funchal have the same number series as those travelling routes outside the city, so it is best to verify your destination before boarding, which is at the front of the bus. Buses run all the week and quite late at night, though there is some reduction of service on Sundays and public holidays. Details of the more popular bus routes are often shown in the reception area of hotels and couriers will be able to advise you about day trips.

If you are taking a long bus ride be prepared for much undulation, bends, and jolting on some country roads. This can be very exhausting, but the scenery makes the journey worthwhile.

Coach excursions

One of the best ways to explore Madeira's hilly terrain and narrow roads is by taking a coach tour. These outings are well advertised in hotels, travel agents and local newspapers. Half day, whole day and evening trips should be booked in advance. The tour operator couriers in your hotel will have all the latest details and prices. It is a good idea to check that your coach will have an English-speaking guide on board and to find out whether a meal is included in the cost. If not, then you will probably be able to arrange for your hotel to give you a packed lunch box. Perhaps you will enjoy your drive more if you take a can of lemonade or some boiled sweets to calm you as you go round sharp steep bends! Remember to take sunglasses, sunhat, cardigan or raincoat when going to the mountains. Sturdy footwear is essential as many places have cobbled streets. Some eau de cologne impregnated face tissues can be refreshing.

It is more than likely that you will make a stop for souvenir shopping, so have some extra escudos with you. At the larger shops, such as the wicker work factory at Camache, credit cards like Visa and Access are accepted.

It is normal practice to tip the coach driver 100 escudos at the end of the tour; you will feel it is well earned after you have travelled along the coast road and in the mountains.

Some of the excursions that can be made are:

- **Island tour** Drive along the south coast, past fishing villages, to the north and west coasts.
- **Simply Madeira** See the high cliffs and stunning scenery of tiny farms in terraced valleys. Visit fishing villages and forests.
- **Venture east** Visit a fresh water trout hatchery. See the unique thatched cottages at Santana and the wonderful seascapes down to Machico where Zarco, the explorer, first landed.

Each of the above excursions takes a full day and costs around 4,600 escudos (£20) including lunch.

The following are half-day excursions:

- **The Blandy Gardens** A delightful stroll around the Quinta at Palheiro Ferreiro, with its gracious house and tropical gardens. Then taste some Madeiran wine at a lodge in Funchal. About 1,700 escudos (£7.39).
- **The levada walk** The coach will take you to the start of a walk and a guide will go with you amongst majestic scenery and the clear air in the mountains. The coach will then pick you up and return you to your hotel. About 2,200 escudos (£9.56).
- **The nuns' hideaway** A visit to the area where the nuns fled from raiding pirates into the hidden village of Curral das Freiras. About 2,000 escudos (£8.69).
- **The crater and toboggan tour** You are taken to the Pico dos Barcelos to enjoy an excellent view of Funchal, then on to Monte and the fun of the famous toboggan ride down to Funchal. It's quite a bumpy experience! About 3,000 escudos (£13), excluding toboggan ride.
- **The espetada evening** The coach takes you out to Funchal to a typical Madeiran restaurant where you enjoy *espetada,* beef with herbs grilled over an open fire and served on huge skewers. You will be entertained by laughing folk dancers and their delightful children. About 3,200 escudos (£13.90).

Children under 12 are usually charged half price on excursions. Travel agents with whom you can book excursions are:

— **Secol Thomson Holidays** Tel: 46948/42241 or speak to any Thomson representative.
— **Agencia Viagens Savoy** Avenida do Infante, Funchal Tel: 31151/22031
— **Blandy** Avenida do Mar 1, Funchal Tel: 20161
— **Atlantica De Luxe Tours** Rua dos Ferreiros 177, Funchal. Tel: 25134
— **Cat** Avenida Arriaga 62, Funchal. Tel: 23966
— **Euromar** Avenida do Infante 58, Funchal. Tel: 20152
— **Panorama,** Rua Dr J Brito Câmara 3, Funchal. Tel: 29194
— **Windsor Estrada Monumental 254, Funchal. Tel: 31057**

Boat trips

As well as coach excursions you can take a sea excursion for a half or whole day, often with swimming included. When the sea is calm the boats will go close inshore so that in the clear waters you can see giant boulders and volcanic lava rocks, and you can observe many sea birds among the high cliffs of the coastline. Popular sea excursions are:

- **Full day boat trip** Lunch is included. About 7,000 escudos (£30.40).
- **Island hopping** Sail across to Porto Santo and tour the island, then soak up the sun and have a swim on a glorious unspoilt beach. About 9,000 escudos (£39).

Boat excursions can be booked with Amigos do Mar, whose office is opposite the yacht marina in Funchal.

This modern ferry plys between Madeira and Porto Santo.

One of Madeira's unique features, the Levada walks take one into the countryside. Stout footwear is required.

Levada walks

Madeira is a volcanic and mountainous country, and when the early settlers started to farm the land they had to resort to very extensive terracing of the steep countryside in order to get level surfaces. At the same time they had to solve the problem of irrigating the land they had prepared. Madeira has plenty of water, as the prevailing north and northeast winds catch the central mountain chain, bringing clouds and rain. The rain would sweep down the steep ravines and into the sea were it not for the porous volcanic ash and basalt clay which collects some of this deluge into water wells. However, these natural springs are high up in the mountains so a system had to be devised to bring the water down to the cultivated lower and warmer slopes on the southern side of the island.

As early as 1461 saw the beginning of the *levada* system, a series of manmade channels and tunnels designed to bring the water flow to the agricultural terraces and into the tilled furrows for the plants. All the *levadas* were built by hand, using stones and clods of earth; sometimes the areas were so difficult of access that men had to be suspended by ropes over the sides of cliffs, then with only crude implements had to hack away at the ground surface to form a channel. In more accessible places a path or steps were made alongside these waterways in order to maintain them. It is these tracks and paths that now form the important tourist attraction, the *levada* walks. Some of these paths are now bordered with trees, shrubs and flowers and all give spectacular views of the magnificent and green countryside.

Many of these walks are suitable for everyone, so long as they are wearing stout footwear. But others are more arduous and can be dangerous, even for experienced climbers, without a guide. A number of hotels and travel agents organise walks along the *levadas* (see page 38).

Early in the 1900s there were only two hundred *levada* systems, but in 1939 the Portuguese Government began a study to improve the water courses. They decided to incorporate the flow of water through hydro-electric power stations, before releasing it in a controlled flow down the water courses to the areas under cultivation. Today the irrigation system extends along 2,150 km, of which 40 km are tunnels through the mountains, some even flowing under waterfalls. This prodigious work took many years and cost several lives.

Such is the tenacity and determination of the hard working Madeirans who, even today, have few technical tools to work the difficult terrain and maintain those valuable *levadas*. Walking these manmade *levada* paths you can really appreciate the efforts of men to control and harness the elements; at the same time it is a rewarding way to enjoy the beautiful Madeiran landscape.

A pleasant stroll along the Levada walks is an ideal way to enjoy the varied landscape of Madeira.

FIVE

A to Z information for visitors

British Consul

The Honorary British Consul in Madeira, Mr. Richard Blandy, is to be found at the offices of Blandy Brothers, Avenida Zarco 2-4, Funchal. Tel: 21221. It is by the seafront, Avenida do Mar, opposite the yacht marina. Office hours 0900 to 1230.

Churches

Madeira, like Portugal, is almost entirely of the Roman Catholic religion. Mass is said in most of the churches on the island. There are Roman Catholic services said in English in the Igreja do Pena, Funchal on Sunday at 10.30 hrs.

The English church is in the Rua de Quebra Costas 18, Funchal. On Sunday, Holy Communion is at 0800 and 1200 hrs, Matins and a sermon at 1100 hrs. The resident chaplain is always glad to receive visitors and informal refreshments are served after the Sunday morning service, in aid of church funds. The church is rather hidden behind a high wall in a large garden. Inside, the organ dates back to 1841 and was imported from Britain. Churchgoers and visitors always admire the floral arrangements. The church, which is part of the Diocese of the Bishop of Gibraltar, also has a library of over 2,500 books. Should you be interested to see the British cemetery, it is higher up the Rua da Carreira. Visitors are welcome. Some of the early gravestones commemorate the many sick people who came to Madeira because of its mild climate.

The Baptist Church in Funchal is at Alto Pena, between Rua Pedro José Ornelas and Rua Sidonio Pais and there is an English language service at 1100 hrs on Sundays.

The Tourist Office in Funchal can provide dates and times of religious services for these and other denominations.

Communications

Post

Post offices are indicated by the letters CTT (Correios, Telegrafos e Telefones). Letter posting boxes follow the British design and are painted red.

The main post offices in Funchal are to be found in the Avenida Zarco and Rua Dr Brito Câmara. They are open from Monday to Friday, 0900 to 1900 hrs. There is also one in the tourist area of Lido Sol and at the airport. A mobile post office complete with telephones is on the docks to meet cruise ships.

Visitors can have their mail sent for collection at the main post office. It should be addressed, surname first, to Poste Restante, Estacao de Correijo de Funchal, Avenida Zarco, Funchal, Madeira, Portugal. To collect mail addressed to you your passport must be shown as a means of identification. At the time of writing postage to the UK costs 60 escudos (£0.26) for a letter and 55 escudos (£0.23) for a postcard. Stamps can also be obtained from hotel receptions, tobacconists and some shops. All mail goes by air and can be registered.

Telephones

In the towns automatic telephones *(telefone)* are to be found on the streets. For a local call use a 2, 10, 20, or 25 escudo coin. Add more if your call is to be lengthy as unused coins are returned. Recently, Credifone cards have been introduced (like a credit card). These are available from the post office in units of 25 or 1000 escudos. Telephones in cafés and bars are usually metered and you pay for units used.

International calls can be made through a clerk at the post office or in your hotel. During the summer months the lines are busy and lengthy delays are to be expected. The dialling code for the UK is 00-44, then the subscriber's code and number. In the case where the code starts with 0 this is omitted. For example, for London (01), just dial 1. It is cheaper to phone the UK between 2000 and 0800 hrs.

In Funchal an easy method of making a telephone call is to go to the main post office in Avenida Zarco; there you have a numbered booth, and you dial your number and pay at the desk after your call.

Telegraph

Telegrams may be sent from the post office in Funchal at Avenida de Zarco, Rua Dr Joáo de Brito Câmara, Rua do Arcipreste and Estrada Monumental 308. You may also send telegrams abroad at the Marconi Company, Avenida Arriaga (near the Cathedral), which is open seven days a week. Tel: 20011. Some hotel receptions will send telegrams.

Telex

The main post office in Avenida de Zarco, Funchal, is the only office that has facilities for sending and receiving telex. Some hotels and travel agents will accept telex using their own telex number. Fax machines are gradually becoming more plentiful.

Currency and banks

Madeira is part of Portugal and therefore the currency is the escudo. 100 centavos compose one escudo, which is written 1$00. There are notes for 5,000, 1,000, 500, 100 and 50 escudos, and coins for 50, 25, 20, 10, 5, 2.5, 1 and .5 escudos. A conto is 1,000 escudos. Higher priced items are often quoted in contos, a point to be observed when shopping.

There is no limit to the amount of foreign currency that can be brought into Madeira; at present no more than 50,000 escudos per person may be taken into Madeira, but regulations also require a visitor to have a minimum of 10,000 escudos on arrival and an additional amount of 2,000 escudos (or equivalent in other currencies) for each day of their intended stay.

The 'high street' banks in Madeira have names like Banco Borges, Banco Espirito Santo and Banco Nacional Ultra Marino; most are in Funchal and found in Avenido Arriago. These Portuguese banks are represented in London. There is a bank at the Airport Santa Catarina.

Most banks accept Eurocheques (with encashment cards) and international credit cards. When you go to a bank you will need to show your passport. Banks are open from 0830 to 1145 and 1300 to 1445 hrs Monday to Friday. The currency exchange rate is displayed in banks, travel agents and hotels, where you may also cash traveller's cheques and change currency. A small commission is charged for this transaction. International credit cards are generally accepted in hotels, restaurants and large shops. Hotels usually have deposit boxes for guests to secure their valuables. Madeirans are generally law abiding, but it is sensible to take precautions against pickpockets, especially in market places.

Duty free allowances

The duty free allowance into the UK is:
— 300 cigarettes or 75 cigars or 400g of tobacco
— 5 litres of still wine
— 1½ litres of spirits over 22% or 3 litres below 22% (eg fortified or sparkling wine) or a further 3 litres of wine
— 90cc of perfume
— 375cc of toilet water
— £250 worth of other goods (but no more than 50 litres of beer and 25 mechanical lighters)

Visitors to Madeira over the age of 17 years, may take the following goods into the country free:
— 1 bottle of spirits
— 2 bottles of table wine
— 200 cigarettes or 250g of tobacco
— ¼ litre of toilet water
— 50g of perfume

It is forbidden to take fresh meat into Madeira. Small quantities of tea and coffee for personal use only may be taken in.

Electricity

Electricity is supplied at 220 volts, 50 cycles. You will require a two-pin plug or a continental adaptor to use electrical equipment.

Fire precautions

Fire precautions are observed in Madeira, with public buildings, including hotels, being inspected for adequate fire escape equipment. Fire emergency instructions should be displayed in your hotel or apartment block.

Modern fire fighting equipment is located in Funchal.

The emergency telephone number to call the Fire Fighting Services is 115. They can also be contacted on 29116 and 22122.

Hairdressing

Men's barbers are called *barbeiros,* women's and unisex salons *cabeleireiros.* A man's haircut costs 400 escudos (£1.74) and a lady's cut and blow dry 1,500 escudos (£6.52), shampoo and set 1,300 escudos (£5.65). The larger hotels have hairdressing salons with modern equipment where the staff understand English.
Women's hairdressers in Funchal are:
— **Amadeu** Rua do Bom Jesus 4-1. Tel: 27627
— **Avenida** Avenida Arriaga 30-2. Tel: 30485
— **Capucine** Buganvilea -C Velho da Ajuda. Tel: 32644
— **Cabbelli** Centro Comercial do Infante. Tel: 29429
— **Katy** Estrada Monumental 308. Tel: 22637
— **Mónaco** Rua do Aljube 7-1. Tel: 22407
— **Michelle** Rua Imperatriz D. Amelia. Tel: 64945
— **Top Style** Estrada Monumental 316. Tel: 30842

Health

There are no dangerous animals or poisonous reptiles on Madeira or Porto Santo. At times flies and mosquitoes are a nuisance, especially when it is warm and has been raining, so it's a good idea to arm yourself with a cream repellent. The Atlantic climate here is generally a healthy one, sea breezes move the air on most days, even during the summer when it rarely gets extremely hot. In the winter it is never extremely cold, except high in the mountains where it can snow; usually the greatest health problem to visitors is caused by over indulgence of different types of food and drink and probably too much time spent lying in the hot sunshine.

Care must be taken to ensure that salads and fruit are quite clean before being consumed. In Madeira there is plenty of fresh and pure mountain water in the taps that is safe to drink but if there is any doubt in your mind about this, cheap and pleasant to drink bottled water can be purchased from bars and supermarkets. Aerated water is called *agua com gás* and still is *agua sem gás.* A 1½ litre bottle costs about 80 escudos (£0.34). It is advisable not to drink tap water in Porto Santo.

Cases of upset tummy or diarrhoea are not to be expected but should these occur avoid alcoholic drinks and salads. A chemist should be consulted to obtain a suitable medication; chemist shops *(farmacias)* are open during normal business hours, and, as in the UK, there is a rota of those that are open outside these hours. Your hotel reception should be able to advise you. There is an English chemist in the centre of Funchal: Botica Inglesa, Avenida Zarco (near the post office).

A health service information centre for tourists is found in Rua das Pretas, Funchal. Modern health centres are in other parts of the island and on Porto Santo. Telephone numbers are given in the **Doctors** section, below.

Avoid too much exposure of the body to the sun; beware especially of falling asleep whilst sunbathing. The wearing of sunglasses, hats and the early use of suntan lotion or cream is sensible. Do not wait until the skin is turning red, that may be too late. Sunstroke can be very distressing. Symptoms are a very severe headache, vomiting and much physical discomfort. Mild cases require a cool shaded room with plenty of liquid to drink (lemonade is helpful). Apply calomine or similar cream to parts affected by the sun. If the skin is blistered or if symptoms are not improving, do not hesitate to consult a health centre, doctor or chemist. Hotel receptions have addresses and telephone numbers.

Great care should be taken if visiting Porto Santo between July and August, as it can be very hot there and there is very little shade from the sun.

Medical insurance

It is advisable to take out personal medical insurance when travelling abroad. This can be arranged through your travel agent, tour operator or insurance company. In addition, British visitors should be in possession of form E111 when visiting Madeira (Portugal belongs to the EEC), obtainable from your local Department of Health and Social Security. This will enable you to receive emergency medical treatment whilst in Madeira, under a bilateral agreement between Portugal and the UK. Without this or personal medical insurance, treatment can be expensive. If you require medical treatment whilst in Madeira and wish to use your form E111, it will be necessary to present it at the office, Servico Migrantes, Rua das Pretas 1, Funchal. Tel: 32021.

Doctors

There are English-speaking medical practitioners in Madeira and a well-equipped general hospital in Funchal, as well as good private clinics. Note that there is no hospital on Porto Santo, though there is a medical centre.

The cost of a visit to a doctor or a consultation could be about 1,500 escudos (£6.52) and payment is required at the time of the visit, with further costs for any subsequent treatments. It is advisable to set aside some escudos in case you should need them in an emergency at a time when the banks are not open or it is difficult to change money. Do not forget to ask the doctor for a receipt of payment for the purpose of an insurance claim: they are used to supplying them.

Hotels have addresses and telephone numbers of doctors but in an emergency telephone 115. Some useful telephone numbers and addresses are:

— **Dr Fernando Borges** Rua 31 de Janeiro 75-3, Funchal. Tel: 20454, private residence 63404.

— **Dr António Ribeiro** Rua Câmara Pestana 11-1, Funchal. Tel: 23737, private residence 20441.

— **Dr Francis Zino** Rua do Jasmineiro 6, Funchal. Tel: 42227, private residence 63292.

— **Hospital Regional Cruz de Carvalho** Avenida Luís de Camões, Funchal. Tel: 42111.

— **Centro de Saúde** (Medical Centre) Estrado do Penedo, Porto Santo. Tel: 982211

Dentists

Dentists are fully qualified, their service is good and they use modern equipment. Generally, as a tourist you can call at the surgery and take your turn. Either the dentist or his receptionist will speak some English. Be sure that your personal holiday insurance covers you for emergency dental treatment. As with doctors, dental treatment has to be paid for as received. A receipt for your insurance claim is given. Dental surgeons to be found in Funchal include:

— **Dr Marcos Freire** Rua do Seminário 7-2. Tel: 29110.

— **Dr Charles Vidal** and **Dr Tito Cabral** Noronha Rua dos Murças 42-2. Tel: 30127.

— **Dr João Cardoso** Rua Mercés 15. Tel: 20333.

In tourist areas the hotel reception or your tour representative will know where nearest dentist is located.

Opticians

Opticians provide a reliable service. In Funchal they are able to test your vision and supply spectacles at short notice. In some cases you can claim on your insurance for broken or lost lenses, therefore a

receipt needs to be obtained for work carried out. Opticians in Funchal include:
— **Casa dos Óculos** Rua do Carmo 24-A. Tel: 28458
— **Central** Rua Joao Tavira 29. Tel: 23496
— **Symphrónio** Rua Joao Gago 14. Tel: 22962
— **Óptica Suissa** Rua Câmara Pestana 12. Tel: 22924

Laundry and dry cleaning

All hotels operate a laundry service and dry cleaning can be arranged. In Funchal you will find laundries and dry cleaners at:
— **Brasileira** Rua do Carmo 33A. Tel: 24686
— **Donini** Rua das Pretas 48. Tel: 24406
— **Primaz** Rua 31 de Janeiro 66. Tel: 26787
— **Suprema** Rua João de Deus 2B. Tel: 20438

It is advisable to ascertain that your garment will be ready before you are due to leave the island.

Newspapers and books

English daily and Sunday newspapers can be obtained in Funchal, at the airport, tourist shops and hotels, usually on the day following publication. The cost is about double the UK price. *The Times* costs 225 escudos (£0.98) and the *Daily Express* 125 escudos (£0.54). There is a selection of popular foreign magazines to choose from and English paperbacks if you are prepared to pay the higher prices.

To find out about local events read the *Jornal da Madeira* or *Diário de Noticias* (in Portuguese). The English *Madeira Island Bulletin* has local information and features to interest visitors; it is a free issue and usually available in hotels.

The English book shop Patio, Rua de Carreira 43, Funchal, has a good selection of books and literature.

Philately

For collectors of stamps Madeira has much to offer, both in the way of shops that specialise in philately and the number of particularly beautiful stamps issued. Many have regional motifs, monuments, flowers, folklore and landscapes. When a cruise ship docks, the special mobile post office van is parked alongside the vessel so that letters can have Madeira stamps showing the day of arrival. Special collectors' issues are on sale. The van is also equipped with a public telephone.

Specialist philatelic shops in Funchal are:

— **Centro Filatelico da Madeira** Rua 31 Janeiro 39. Tel: 30084

— **Filatelia Numistmatica da Madeira** Avenida Arriaga 75. Tel: 23070

— **Loja de Filatelia** Avenida Zarco (post office) Tel: 33574

— **Pavilháo de Filatelia** Praça da Restauracao. Tel: 30966

First day issues are obtainable from the main post office in Funchal and at the airport, Câmara de Lobos, Machico, Ribeira Brava and Porto Santo.

Whenever a cruise ship docks at Funchal, this post office van arrives.

Police

The police wear blue uniforms in towns and are responsible for traffic control and for maintaining public order. In Funchal some wear red arm bands marked *Turismo*. This means that they can speak foreign languages and are available to assist tourists. In rural areas the police wear brown uniforms. Nowadays there are quite a number of policewomen to be seen on duty.

To call for police assistance telephone 115. This emergency number is also used to call the ambulance or the fire service.

Problems and complaints

The best place to go if you have a complaint about your accommodation which you have not been able to sort out with the hotel reception, hotel manager or tour operator representative is the Tourist Office, Avenida Arriaga 18, Funchal. In extreme case of distress it may be necessary to go to the police or the British Consul.

Public conveniences

Public conveniences as known in the UK are not very often seen in Madeira or Porto Santo. In Funchal there is a WC at the indoor market, at the eastern end of the Avenida do Mar and there is one on the corner of Avenida M. Arriaga and Avenida Zarco — however, these are best avoided if possible. Generally the public use the facilities provided by a bar, café, restaurant or hotel. It is not necessary to be a customer, but they prefer it when you are. Pictographs such as shoe, hat or figure on the door are often used to show ladies *(senhora)* and gentlemen *(cavalheiro)*.

Radio

Madeira has three radio stations, one of which broadcasts local news and information in English, daily (except Saturday) from 1745 to 1830 hrs, followed by a bulletin of world news. The World Service of the BBC can also be received on SW radio.

Shopping

Shopping in Madeira is very much like shopping in the UK and Europe. Goods usually have a fixed price and are not tax free. Even in the smaller supermarkets you will find someone who understands English. In Funchal there are no big superstores but there are three large shopping centres:

— **Centro Comercial Infante** Avenida Arriaga 73.
— **Centro Comercial Da Sé** Avenida Dr Antonio J Almeida 2.
— **Centro Comercial São Pedro** Rua de São Pedro 37.

Most shops and offices are open Monday to Friday from 0900 to 1300 hrs and from 1500 to 1900 hrs and on Saturday from 0900 to 1300 hrs. The shopping centre in Avenida Arriaga is open from 1000 to 2000 hrs, seven days a week including holidays, and has a restaurant open until midnight. Most of the larger shops accept international credit cards.

Funchal's main market is called **Mercado dos Lavradores** and is full of noise and colour, with flowersellers in native costume. Huge piles of fruit and vegetables, mostly grown locally, are reasonably priced and very fresh. The fish stalls are located in a separate area downstairs. Look for the famous Madeiran fish called *espada,* a horrid looking long, black eel-like fish. Although it looks vicious, when cooked it is surprisingly delicate, with soft white flesh.

Funchal is a pleasant city to shop in even if you have to sometimes walk uphill and one narrow street looks similar to the next. Shopkeepers are used to tourist questions and keep remarkably patient when being asked for directions.

Buying clothes locally

Funchal has a good selection of clothes shops, which range from high class boutiques to rather old-fashioned looking clothing emporiums. Prices range widely and vary according to the shopping area. Modern jeans and tops are very much in evidence in the tourist resorts, hand-embroidered blouses and sportswear too. Children's and baby clothes are often attractive and cheerful. Beachwear, lightweight shoes and sunhats can be purchased from shops near hotels.

Should you wish to purchase a man's suit, alterations can be made within a few hours. It is useful to check your continental metric size before going shopping. The Portuguese word for sale is *saldos;* cheaper is *mais barato* and better is *melhor* (See vocabulary).

Souvenirs

A popular way of buying souvenirs is first to watch them being made. Embroidery and wickerwork are two crafts where you can watch the local people at work and then make a purchase.

Boots At one time boots were worn by the villagers and they are still worn by the folkdancers. Sheepskin boots are on sale at many of the souvenir shops and stalls.

Embroidery Madeiran lace and embroidery are renowned. Although quite expensive any piece purchased will become a family heirloom. Watch that it carries the seal of Ibatam (Instituto do Bordado Tapecarias e Artesanato da Madeira), which guarantees that it has been inspected for quality. You can watch embroiderers at the Ibatam in Funchal and make a purchase. Shops which sell embroideries are Blue Bird at Avenida Arriaga 32 and Casa Nicola at Avenida Arriaga 11.

Flowers There are specialist flower shops that will box flowers ready for you to take home with you on the aircraft. You may take back bulbs and seeds into the UK, too, provided there is no soil with them. Flowers that last well and are worth bringing home are the strelitzias (bird of paradise), orchids and anthuriums (flame flower). A shop that provides a flower packing service is: Multi Flora, Rua da Carreira 118, Funchal.

Musical instrument A very unusual souvenir which can be purchased in various sizes is a *brinquinho,* the percussion instrument adorned by brightly dressed dolls that clap their hands, and used by the folk dancing groups.

The 'brinquinho' has wooden dolls with castenets and bells which make a percussion sound.

Pottery and porcelain If packed carefully in between clothes, gaily painted tiles and ornaments make cheerful souvenirs. The Portuguese national symbol, the Red Cockerel, makes a bright ornament. It comes in many sizes. The legend from the Portuguese town of Barcelos tells of a man accused of stealing who was brought before a judge who sat eating his dinner. The accused man cried his innocence, saying that the rooster in the dish would crow as a sign of the truth — and sure enough the cock did crow. This fascinating story is perpetuated by the colourful cock made in ceramics or wood and seen everywhere in Portugal and Madeira.
Straw hats Old-fashioned boaters, as worn by the toboggan men of Monte, make practical sunhats and good souvenirs.
Tapestry Like the local embroidery these pieces are expensive, as they are laboriously handmade. Often the article depicts one of the old Flemish paintings. Canvases and embroidery materials can be purchased for you to sew your own, if you wish. Tapestries can be purchased at Madeira Gobelins, Rua da Carreira 194.
Wickerwork Various items of this handicraft can be taken home on your aircraft, but don't buy anything larger than a linen basket! Planes flying out of Madeira have a special place in the hold for these articles. So it is not necessary to try and put them in your suitcase. Camacha Wickerwork at Centro Commercial do Infanta is one place to watch skilled people at work and to shop for these items.
Wine The famous Madeira wine makes a most acceptable souvenir or gift. The wine stores will pack you a set of bottles, large or small, to carry home.
Woollen garments The Madeiran workman's woollen hat with bobble and earflaps is sold to tourists as well, and the thick Portuguese wool jumpers and cardigans wear very well and are reasonably priced.
The **Casa do Turista** located in a gracious old house behind the theatre in Funchal, has a wide choice of high class embroidery, wickerwork, ceramics and Madeiran wine for sale.

Television

Madeira is on the Radio Televisaô Portuguesa network and receives one channel from Portugal. There are programmes in English that include films. Video cassettes are now as popular in Funchal as elsewhere in Europe.

Time

Time is the same in Madeira and Portugal as in the UK. The clocks change by one hour for summer and winter at the end of March and October.

Tipping

Tipping is expected, as in the UK and the continent. In bars, cafés and restaurants (except where a service charge may be added to the bill) a tip in the region of 10 per cent may be given, perhaps less for a drink at a bar. Maids and porters handling luggage should be tipped. Taxi drivers expect a 10 per cent tip, but generally the Madeirans are well mannered and do not make much of the subject.

Tobacco and cigarettes

The cost of imported tobacco is about three times more than the products manufactured on the island. Local brands of cigarettes are called Bingo, Goldflame and Magos and cost about 110 escudos (£0.47) a packet. There are also pipe tobaccos. Smoking is not allowed in buses, theatres, cinemas and some taxis.

(Opposite) *This attractive windmill is still in use, near the village of Camacha on the island of Porto Santo.*

SIX

Food and drink

Madeira is a small island in the Atlantic and some way from Europe and North Africa, but nevertheless it offers a variety of food and drink. This is a stopping place for travellers en route to many parts of the trading world and, in addition, since Victorian times it has been popular with wealthy visitors, so it is used to catering for a wide range of tastes. Madeira's normal cuisine is now of a high standard.

Buying food

Prices of household commodities are on a par with most European countries and nowadays many of the well known brand names such as Nescafé and Pepsi Cola, are evident though they are more expensive than in the UK.

Visitors to Madeira who are in self-catering apartments will have no problem buying foodstuffs. As in most countries these days, the ubiquitous supermarket has plenty of stock, all of which is weighed and priced. Shop assistants are friendly in a quiet way; they are used to coping with tourist enquiries and most understand English.

Meat Fresh and frozen meat is plentiful, with beef steak *(bife)* being excellent. Lamb *(borrego),* chicken *(frango)* and rabbit *(coelho)* are on sale at the market in Funchal and in butcher's shops and supermarkets.

Fish This is very popular with the local population. Fresh fish is bought early in the day. In the outlying districts a fishmonger drives to the centre of the village. Supermarkets have frozen sole *(linguado),* shellfish *(mariscos),* sea bream *(besugo)* and hake *(pescaoa).*

(Opposite) *The national costume of Madeira is nowadays worn for folk dancing displays.*

Bread Several varieties of bread *(pao)* are baked. Look out for the crusty *pao com quijo,* which is a small loaf of bread baked with cheese inside. It's very tasty to have as a picnic sandwich.
Cakes These are sold in the *pastelaria.* Madeirans seem to have a sweet tooth and, like the Spanish, often go into a cake shop and buy a creamy cake to eat while they walk in the street.
Fresh salads, fruit and vegetables These are of excellent quality. Large crops of potatoes, broad beans, onions and tomatoes are grown locally and supply the hotels and restaurants. All about the island are banana plantations. The Madeiran banana is the *musa cavendishi,* similar to that grown in the Canary Islands: this banana is small and sweet and is often known as the Demerara banana, the plant having been first introduced to the island from the British Colony of that name in 1842. Other fruits that grow well are the papaya (paw paw) and the avocado, both from the Americas. The former is in season from June to October and the avocado between November and May. Another exotic fruit is the passion fruit *(maracuja),* also called the granadilla. (A real favourite of ours is passion fruit mousse, a speciality of the Sheraton Hotel O Churrasco Grill.) Mangos, custard apples and melons are grown in Porto Santo. Apples, pears, cherries, figs, grapes, lemons, oranges and even strawberries are grown in Madeira's rich soil.

Local dishes

The Madeiran people enjoy their meals and spend a lot of time socialising while they are eating, especially at weekends and on public holidays. At these times best clothes are worn and families get together to meet relations and friends. Madeira has a variety of traditional dishes which you may want to try.
Caldo verde A soup made with potatoes and finely shredded cabbage to which sausage is sometimes added.
Canja de galinha This is a chicken soup with spaghetti, sometimes served early on New Year's Day.
Tomate e cebola com ovo Tomato and onion soup with a poached egg in the centre.
Caldeirada Originally Portuguese, this is a rich mixed fish stew cooked with olive oil, potatoes, onions, tomatoes and bread. You eat the soupy part first, then the fish. Excellent.
Bif de atun Tuna steak, a solid satisfying fish, usually served with boiled potatoes or rice and vegetables.

Will this be your first close look at a hand of bananas?

Espada The popular scabbard fish can be grilled, stewed in wine or fried. It is a soft, flaky fish and always tasty.
Carne de vinho e alphos Pork marinated in wine and garlic, then fried. Served with new potatoes and slices of orange and lemon.
Espetada Chunks of meat, usually beef, which is put on metal or (traditionally) laurel wood skewers and cooked over wood and leaves from the bay tree. This crispy, smoky meat is very tasty.
Bolo de caco A country bread made with flour and sweet potatoes then cooked on a hot stone in a wood burning stove. It is eaten hot with meat dishes.
Inhame cozido Boiled sweet potatoes. (Sweet potatoes are also served fried with chips.)
Milho frito A typical accompaniment to many meals, this is maize or cornmeal flour mixed with lard, water and some herbs, then fried, often in small cubes. Try it for something different.
Bolo de mel Though called a honey cake, this is really made with molasses, fruit and nuts. Traditionally it is a Madeiran Christmas cake. It is rich and dark and keeps very well so makes a tasty souvenir. Most supermarkets and cake shops *(pasteleria)* have them displayed.
Pudim Caramel pudding with a Madeiran wine sauce, similar to the Spanish flan pudding.

Drinks

Madeiran wine, the most well-known drink of the island, is a still, fortified, blended wine that is made only in Madeira. There are four main varieties:

- **Sercial** A pale dry nutty-flavoured wine, produced from Reisling grape vines imported originally from Crete and Germany. The Sercial mellows with age. It's a dry wine which can be served chilled as an aperitif.
- **Verdelho** A rich golden wine with a dry finish. This is an excellent all purpose wine to be served before or after meals, with soup, cake, cheese and nuts.
- **Bual** This is a medium-coloured rich wine, full flavoured, to be served as a dessert wine after meals.
- **Malmsey** The best known of the Madeiras, this is a rich and luscious wine with a fine bouquet. Malmsey is a sweet dessert wine that can be enjoyed before and after meals. The vines of the Malmsey grape need a dry soil and intense heat and the grapes have

to become sun dried almost like raisins before they are gathered.

It is said that Prince Henry the Navigator first introduced the *malvasi candida* vine to Madeira. There is an interesting story telling that when the wine was shipped across the equator the flavour improved noticeably, so nowadays heated chambers and pipes are used to enhance the quality.

Today the Madeira Wine Company, which includes many British names, has a permanent stock of about 10,000 pipes of wine. Touring the wine houses in Funchal is an interesting and popular excursion for many visitors, who can then sample several wines before making a purchase. Madeira does not produce any table wine for export.

There's a good selection of Portuguese wines to choose from when ordering a meal — for example: Almeirim, a white wine with high alcoholic content; Bairrada, red and white sparkling wines; Carcavelos a powerful and distinctive wine; Mateus Rosé, a light red or white sparkling wine; Vinho Verde, the green grape wine with a dry flavour, which can be red or white and is excellent with fish. Sparkling wines *(espumante)* from Portugal can be drunk on many occasions; they come as pink *(rosé),* dry *(seco),* medium dry *(meio secoi),* extra dry *(bruto)* and sweet *(dolce).* A popular and cheap one is Raposeira Reserva from the region of the old city of Lamego.

Brandy from Portugal is called *aguardente,* and there are several varieties having distinctive flavours, such as the Medronho and the Moscatel brandy, which has the flavour of the muscatel grape. The local *Aguardente,* made from sugar cane, is fiery and very potent. One drink to beware of is Poncho, made with lemons, sugar and *aguardente.*

Port, the most favoured of drinks from Portugal, is a drink for all hours of the day or night. Whether it be sweet, medium dry or dry, it can be drunk on its own or chilled and served with lemon or soda water.

Soft drinks such as Coca Cola and Seven-Up are plentiful and bottled mineral waters can be found in all the supermarkets and bars. You should try Maracujá, which is a fizzy drink made from the juice of the passion fruit. Remember that tap water is perfectly safe to drink also though it is not recommended on Porto Santo.

There are 'espresso' machines everywhere, but if you find the coffee (cafe) served in a bar or restaurant too strong, it is quite in order to ask for *um nescafe.* Black coffee in a small cup is *uma bica; uma chinesa* is coffee with milk in a large cup.

Should you wish for tea *(cha)* you can expect to get a tea bag, sugar or lemon, so ask for *com leite* if you require milk with tea.

Using the bars, cafés and restaurants

Bars, cafés and snack bars are in abundance in Madeira and are very much a way of life. They often open quite early in the morning and stay open very late or until the last customer has gone. These establishments all serve alcohol, coffee, soft drinks and snacks, some even serve meals long after restaurants have closed. The Prince Albert and Joe's bar behind the Savoy Hotel and near the Madeira Sheraton are popular with the younger tourists in the Funchal area. Open air cafés are very popular with holidaymakers who can sit in the glorious sunshine enjoying a coffee or beer. You may sit at your table as long as you wish and it is not necessary to pay for your drinks until you are about to leave.

Restaurants serve lunch generally between 1200 and 1500 hrs, with dinner from 1900 to 2300 hrs. But there are a number that serve meals all day. Funchal is unique in having every variety of cuisine from luxury grill rooms to simple typical Portuguese fish restaurants. One of the nicest ways of observing the locals is to have a meal in a backstreet restaurant in Funchal.

Many restaurants advertise in the *Madeira Island Bulletin* (a tourist newspaper issued free) and the tour representative in your hotel or apartment block will be pleased to recommend nearby eating establishments. Remember that you may eat in a hotel restaurant, even if you are not staying there. Another way to choose a restaurant is to ask a fellow guest or traveller on a coach excursion, who may have discovered just the type of place to suit you.

When in Funchal you will discover that the large shopping centres such as the Centro Comercial Infante. Avenida Arriaga 73, have a number of snack bars, cafés and restaurants, but remember they are often busy with local office workers at lunchtime. Most restaurants accept international credit cards.

Restaurants in Funchal

Expensive

Caravela Avenida do Mar 15. Upstairs, with a splendid view over the harbour.

Golfinho Largo de Corpo Santo 21. In old part of city. Sea food.

Kon Tiki Rua do Favilla 9. Reservations required. Interesting food.
Romano Largo do Corpo Santo 15. In the old part of the city. Top quality food.
Taverna Real Off Rua Fernao de Ornelas. Madeiran and Austrian food in a splendidly restored fifteenth century cellar. Fado only at dinner. Closed on Sunday.

Moderately priced

A Rampa Avenida Infante Edificio Henrique 11- 1A. International and Italian cuisine.
A Seta Estrada do Livramento 80. On the outskirts of the city. Recommended.
Brisa Estrada Dr João Abel De Freitas 104. North of the city. Typical local dishes.
Carochinha Rua de São Francisco 2A. English restaurant serving roast beef.
Espadarte Estrada da Boa Nova 5. Good, friendly place serving *espetada* (skewered meat). Sometimes fado and folk dancing.
Patio Avenida Zarco 21. Right in the city. Next door to the English Bookshop. Outdoor tables in an old-fashioned, elegant setting.
Tahiti Rua das Pretas 19. Small and friendly, with local foods.

Inexpensive

A Flor Rua da Quemada de Baixo. Regional food. Used by Madeirans.
A Gruta Estrada da Pontinha. A cave in old walls overlooking the harbour, with an outdoor patio.
A Marisqueira Infante Shopping Centre. Small, clean and air-conditioned.
Apolo In Cathedral Square. Good, generous meals.
Estrella do Mar Largo do Corpo Santo 1-7. Delicious food; sea food and lobster tanks.
Gavina's Rua do Gorgulho, near Lido. Simple sea food. With a sea view.
Joe's Snack Bar Rua Penha da Franca. In the garden of Albergaria Quinta da Penha da Franca. Serves salads and light meals. Friendly place, open in the evening.
O Bau Estrada Monumental. Near Hotel Girassol. Small. Serves local food.

The Apolo Restaurant with its outdoor tables is a good meeting place in Funchal.

Restaurants around Madeira

Camacha

Café Relogio Regional Dishes. Moderately priced.

Camara do Lobos

Coral Bar Fresh fish and salads. Moderately priced.
Ribamar Regional food. Moderate prices.

Canico

A Lareira In square by the church. Local food with pleasant service. Moderately priced.
O Boiero Local specialities and steaks. Expensive.
Restrante Central Good meat dishes. Moderately priced.

Faial

Casa de Chá do Faial Well cooked regional food in country setting. Moderate prices.

Machico

Facho Excellent local dishes. Moderate prices.
Luigi Real Italian food. Moderate prices.
Mercado Velho Good local food. Inexpensive.

Porto Moniz

Cachalote By the sea. Good cooking, and fish dishes. Inexpensive.
Fernandes Used by the coach tours. Good value and service. Moderately priced.

Santa Cruz

Varanda At the airport, with a good view. Moderately priced.

Santana

O Colmo Excellent choice of regional foods. Moderately priced.

Serra de Água

Posada dos Vinháticos Scenic location in the mountains. Expensive.

São Vicente

Galeao Good place for lunch. Inexpensive.

Restaurants in Porto Santo

Although Porto Santo has only one four-star hotel, the local small restaurants provide good quality, especially fresh fish dishes, and the friendly service is pleasant.

Assenios Vila Baleira. Restaurant, fish and paella. Moderately priced.

Baiana. Vila Baleira. Cafe, regional food. Inexpensive.

Gazela Campo de Cima. Restaurant, barbecue meat. Expensive.

Marques Vila Baleira. Restaurant, regional food. Moderately priced.

Porto Santo Hotel Vila Baleira. Restaurant, à la carte, menu, high class decor. Expensive.

Tocado Pescador Ponta da Calheta. Very simple beach café, fresh fish. Moderately priced.

SEVEN

Leisure activities

Walking

Walking is one of the prime pastimes for Madeira's visitors. Whether you are taking a gentle stroll along Funchal's long seafront, toiling up the steep cobbled streets of many villages, or enjoying more ambitious tours of the countryside, walking is surely the best way to enjoy this attractive island. Keep your high-heeled shoes for visits to the Casino — out of doors you'll require comfortable low-heeled footwear, and strong walking shoes or boots for the mountain walks.

There are long and short walks; you can climb Madeira's highest mountain, the Pico Ruivo (1861m/6105ft), or just ramble in the country for an hour or so. Many walks are recommended and trails are shown on maps. The Tourist Office and hotels have details. A useful map is number 7 in the Clyde Leisure Maps Series (obtainable from Stanfords Map Centre, 12 Long Acre, London WC2 — about £2.75). There is an excellent book for walkers called *Landscapes of Madeira,* by John and Pat Underwood (see Bibliography).

Average walkers may like to join some of the organised walking tours. Several of the travel agents have programmes. For example Star Travel in Funchal offer two good, full day excursions.

- The first walk is nine kilometres long in the morning; about two and a half hours along the Levada da Serra Faial to Lamaceiros, with magnificent panoramas over the north west coast. From there you travel by bus to Santo da Serra for lunch. You then walk in the opposite direction along the Levada da Serra to Águas Mansas. It takes about one and a half hours to cover the five kilometres amongst lush green countryside. The cost is 3,800 escudos (£16.52).
- Walk number two starts at Pico do Arieiro (1,810m). You follow a trail linking the island's three highest mountains. Soon you see Pico das Torres (1,851m) to the northwest, further on Pico

Ruivo (1,861m) comes into view; you continue to Pico do Gato and the tunnels. You will have a spectacular view over Pico Grande and the expanse of Pául da Serra. Reaching the resthouse below Pico Ruivo you can stop for a picnic before climbing to the summit. You then descend to Achada do Teixeira, where you are taken by bus to Faial for lunch. The distance from Pico do Arieiro to Pico Ruivo is seven kilometres and takes about three hours. Pico Ruivo to Achada do Teixeira is three kilometres, and takes about forty-five minutes. The cost of this walk is 4,900 escudos (£21.30). A warm jumper, raincoat and stout footwear are essential, possibly a sun hat and sunglasses, too.

The Tourist Office in Funchal has a booklet which lists walks. This has a grading system which shows pictorially one rabbit to denote a walk 'suitable for all ages', two rabbits for a walk 'suitable for walkers accustomed to rough walking in the country'; three rabbits denotes 'many ascents and descents, should be undertaken by experienced walkers'; four rabbits that 'walks of this grade should be undertaken only by experienced walkers accustomed to heights'.

Walkers are advised to obtain information from their hotel porter about weather conditions in the location they intend to walk. You should indicate your time of departure and when you expect to return. The mist on high peaks often appears suddenly, so it is best to walk in groups with one member having an alarm whistle to call help. Remember, too, that dusk turns into a dark night in half an hour.

Sports and pastimes

The mild climate, the mountains, and the proximity of the sea make it possible to participate in a wide selection of sports when in Madeira. There's a choice of more sedentary occupations too.

Bicycling

You can cycle on Madeira, but the enthusiast cannot expect much in the way of satisfaction. The roads are narrow, rough and mountainous, and there are few flat tracks.

Bowling

The facilities for bowling and skittles are limited. The Hotel Vila Ramos in Funchal provides bowling alleys.

The start of the walk from Pico do Arieiro to Pico Ruivo is amid magnificent mountain scenery.

Bridge

In the larger hotels bridge is a popular pastime, and cardrooms and tables are available. Couriers will put you in touch with other visitors who enjoy the game or you may see a notice requesting a partner for a game at a certain time. Many elderly people come to the island especially to play bridge. There is an important bridge club in the Matur Tourist Complex.

Casino

The Casino Park Complex is a short distance from the centre of Funchal with the Casino de Madeira (Tel: 25228) in the Avenida do Infante. The facilities can compete with the world's most famous casinos. Here you can play Crap, Black Jack, Roulette and slot machines. There is an exclusive private gambling room for the really dedicated. The casino is open every day from 1600 to 0300 hrs. There is an entrance fee of 700 escudos in to the gaming rooms only. You will need to produce your passport. After 2000 hrs gentlemen need to wear a tie and jacket. The Casino Park Complex includes a five-star luxury hotel that provides activities such as tennis, table tennis, swimming pool, sauna, massage, gymnasium, billiards and bridge.

Diving

The rocky coasts and clear water make for excellent deep sea diving, snorkelling, skin and skuba diving with further opportunities near the Deserta islands (Ilhas Deserta). Information is available and equipment can be hired at the Inter Atlas Hotel, Garajua, Caniço. Tel: 932421. There is also a Diving Club there.

Fishing

Deep sea fishing is a well established sport and specially equipped boats can be hired. Bluefin, bigeye and longtail tuna can be caught, as well as amverjack, blue marlin, swordfish and a variety of sharks. Equipment is available from the Don Pedro Hotel, Machico. Tel: 962751; Amigos do Mar, Marina do Mar, Funchal. Tel: 042468; and from the Madeira Game Fishing Centre. Fishing from the harbour in Funchal can produce sea bream, sea perch, moray and conger eel.

Football
Football is very much a spectator sport for the Madeirans, who make it a family day out. The local clubs play in league matches with the Portuguese clubs. The largest football stadium is near Quinta Magnolia, close to the hotel district. The more important matches are played on a Sunday.

Golf
There is a nine-hole golf course at Santo da Serra to the north east of Funchal. It is situated midst eucalyptus and mimosa trees and there are fine mountain views. There is a club house and bar. Golf clubs can be hired. The green fees are higher at weekends and at holiday times.

Horse riding
You can enjoy riding at the Centro de Hipismo da Madeira Caminho (just to the west of Funchal). Tel: 24982. It is near the Hotel Estrelicio where you can also make reservations (Tel: 30131). Horses are available daily, except on Saturday and Sunday, from 0930 to 1700 hrs.

Hunting
The season for shooting pigeon, rabbit, quail and partridge is from October to December. The Madeirans love this sport which is carried out in the countryside below the high mountains. If you are interested in joining a shoot, the Tourist Office in Funchal can tell you how to obtain a licence.

Mini golf
There are miniature golf courses at the following places: Atlantis Hotel, Machico; the Savoy, Madeira Sheraton and Vila Ramos hotels in Funchal. You do not need to be a resident to use their facilities.

Sailing
Sailing dingies are used mostly inshore. Arrangements for hiring a boat can be made through the Tourist Office, the Naval Club, Amigos do Mar, Rota do Atlantico, and the Madeira Sheraton, Savoy and Reid's hotels.

Swimming

You can swim all the year round. In summer the water temperature is as high as 20°C (72°F). There are few beaches along Madeira's rocky coast. You can swim in the pools at the Lido, the Club de Turismo and the Naval Club. Porto Moniz has a small natural swimming pool. All the hotels have swimming pools, some are heated when necessary, and there are pools for young children. The island of Porto Santo has a very long beach of golden sand and clear water. Currents around the islands can be dangerous when the sea is rough, so be very careful.

Tennis and squash

The principal hotels have their own tennis courts which are also open to non-residents. The Quinta Magnolia, which is near Reid's Hotel and was once the British Country Club and now taken over as a public park, has tennis courts and a squash court. You can buy tennis and other sports equipment in Funchal.

Wind surfing and water ski

Arrangements to waterski and windsurf can be made at the Reid's and Savoy hotels in Funchal. The Dom Pedro Hotel in Machico has a waterski and windsurfing school. Care must be taken when engaging in watersports when the sea is rough and it is windy as the currents around the islands can be very dangerous.

The golden sands of Porto Santo's beach.

Night life

Most evening activities take place in larger hotels. You do not need to be a resident to take part in the enjoyment of the floor shows.

Some of the typical Madeiran restaurants have folkloric dancing on some evenings. The Casino da Madeira has a nightly floor show in the **Zodiac Night Club,** as well as the Gambling Rooms. The Savoy Hotel has a night club called the **Galaxia** and the Hotel Atlantis (Água de Pena) one called the **Atlantis.** There is a night club called **Safari** in the Rua do Favila 5, Funchal. **Disco Faro** is part of the Madeira Sheraton Hotel and it is open from 2200 to 0300 hrs (closed on Sunday). There is no entrance charge.

In the cafés and restaurants in the old part of the city of Funchal you can still hear traditional Portuguese songs *(fados)* and that is where you will also meet the local population. **Marcelino's** and **Arsenio's** are bars that have late evening *fados.*

There is a municipal **theatre** in Avenida Arriaga as well as **cinemas** in Funchal.

Museums

Museu de Arte Sacre (Sacred Art Museum) Rua do Bispo. Open 1000 to 1230 and 1430 to 1700 hrs, mornings only on Sunday, closed on Monday. This was built in 1600 as the residence of the Bishop of Funchal. Now only the Chapel of St Luis and the northern facade of arcades remain. This section houses the museum and contains valuable religious paintings and vestments. Many of these works of art, which were brought to the island in the fifteenth and sixteenth century, are of Flemish origin and were in payment for sugar shipped from Funchal. The municipal archives are housed in this museum.

Museu da Quinta da Cruzes (Estate of the Cross) Calcada do Pico 1. Open 1000 to 1230 and 1430 to 1700 hrs, Sunday 1000 to 1300 hrs, closed Monday. This ancient and beautiful house is reputed to be on the site where the discoverer of Madeira had his original residence in Funchal. The present building was built during the seventeenth and eighteenth century with additions in the early nineteenth century. Even if you are not particularly keen on museums this one, right in the heart of Funchal, is really worth visiting. It is particularly well laid out and with the aid of a small leaflet issued free at the entrance, you can enjoy an enchanting hour or so looking at bygone treasures. These include collections of beautiful hand-made furniture, silver, china, paintings and works of art from many parts of the world. You are sure to see something of interest — such as a pair of ebony and silver figures of young slave girls, circa second half of the eighteenth century, which are exquisite and a reminder of the time when slaves worked on Madeira's plantations. Maybe you will pause to have a longer look at the strong cupboards made from the boxes used in the sugar trade with Brazil.

Another unusual feature of the Quinta is that in the garden are a number of archaeological objects such as huge carved stone coats-of-arms, ancient tombstones, a Manueline window made of Madeiran basalt. These large objects stand out strangely amongst the exotic trees and plants. There is a large collection of exotic orchids.

Museu Municipal (Municipal Museum and Aquarium) Rua da Mouraria 35. Open 0900 to 1700 hrs, Saturday and Sunday 1200 to 1800 hrs, closed Monday. Said to have been the home of Count Ribeiro Real, this solid town house built in the eighteenth century is now a museum of fauna, geological specimens and birds. A small collection of fish found in the seas around Madeira is downstairs. The building also houses the regional archives.

Museu do Bombeiro (Firemen's Museum) Caminho de Dom João. Equipment and curiosities about firefighting in Madeira since the late nineteenth century.

Photographic Museu Vicente Avenida Zarco. This delightful old building houses a photographic studio museum with nineteenth-century cameras, glass plates and photographs. Open from 1400 to 1800 hrs. Entrance is free.

Wine Museum Rua de Outubro 7. This is where the quality and the production of the island's wine industry is controlled. Part of the building is open to the public and contains historic documents and relics of the wine trade.

EIGHT

Madeira and its people

Historical background

The first visitors

Unlike the Canary Islands, Madeira bears no sign of early aboriginal inhabitants. For many centuries its islands remained undisturbed by mankind, a place of thick forests, its shores occasionally visited by storm-blown sailors. When the Roman historian Pliny came to write in the first century AD of the 'Fortunate Islands' found off the coast of North Africa — by which he meant today's Canary Islands — he also mentioned the 'Purple Islands' to the north, which we know now as the Madeira Archipelago. It is thought that this colourful description derives from the resin of the *drago milenaro,* the dragon tree, a product valued in his day and used to dye clothes and carpets.

A much-favoured legend concerning early visitors to Madeira tells of a fourteenth-century English adventurer named Robert Machim (or Mackean) who fell in love with the beautiful Anne D'Arset (Dorset). Unfortunately she was betrothed to another English nobleman and marriage was unwillingly forced on her. However love soon prevailed and the pair eloped, sailing from Bristol in a ship bound for Brittany. A fearful storm blew their vessel far off course, but after fourteen days adrift in the Atlantic land was sighted. The lovers took refuge on Madeira, delighted to find themselves in a warm, sunny climate. Unfortunately the same storm returned, wrecking their already damaged ship as it lay at anchor. Then Anne became sick and soon died in her lover's arms. Heartbroken, Robert Machim buried his loved one by an altar at the foot of a great tree. He placed a large cedarwood cross nearby with an inscription asking any future Christian settlers to build a church beside Anne's grave. Soon afterwards he himself died, to be buried alongside his beloved.

The story does not end there though, for it is said that the remainder of the ship's crew managed to construct a small boat, eventually sailing to Africa and the Barbary Coast. Here they were captured and sold into slavery, and it was not until their escape to Europe many years later that their tale of a beautiful island with large trees and a warm sun could finally be told. However, this popular story is not based on any historical facts.

The Portuguese arrive

Reports of Madeira eventually reached the Portuguese court, arousing the interest of its great sailors, not least Prince Henry the Navigator, son of King João I. Two explorers, João Goncalves Zarco and Tristao Vaz Teixeira, set sail in search of this green isle and in 1419 came upon a small sandy island, which they named Porto Santo. A year later an Italian, Bartolomeu Perestrello, joined them in a further expedition and finally, in 1420, Madeira was discovered. They arrived at a great bay in the south-east of the island at a place now called Machico, a name that appears to uphold the romantic legend of the unfortunate love of Robert Machim. Today the Capela do Senhor dos Milagres, the Chapel of Miracles, in Machico is said to stand on the site where the original church was built to honour the lovers' graves.

When Zarco set foot on the island he found it covered mostly by thick forest with no sign of inhabitants. After collecting some of the wood and plants he returned with his fleet to the Portuguese Court. Thus the discovery of Madeira is credited to João Goncalves Zarco, with the island receiving the name 'Isla da Madeira', meaning 'island of timber'.

On his return to the archipelago Zarco claimed the islands as a Portuguese colony. He divided Madeira into two parts, taking control of the western half himself and giving the east to his lieutenant Tristao Vaz Teixeira. The third territory, Porto Santo, was administered by Bartolomeu Perestrello.

A thriving Portuguese colony

Zarco proved to be a diligent administrator, constructing houses and establishing plantations. Unfortunately, fires were started in order to clear the land and these often got out of control, destroying great areas of timber. It is said that on parts of the island the fires smouldered for as long as seven years. However the results were of some advantage, for in time the vast amounts of wood ash that remained enriched the soil and helped produce bountiful crops.

In 1425 the first sugar cane was brought from Italy and while the mountainous terrain made cultivation arduous the mild climate proved beneficial. A system of water channels called *levadas* was built, bringing the abundant water supply in the mountains down to the farms and plantations. By 1452 the first sugar mill was established to crush the cane, using this water for power.

As the first settlers prospered, so news of this island of pleasant climate and fertile land reached the noble families of Portugal. The Madeiran economy soon flourished, and the Portuguese population was joined by Jewish merchants and businessmen and adventurers from England, Scotland, Italy and Poland. To help run these new estates slaves were brought over from the Canary Islands and Africa.

Prince Henry the Navigator introduced *malvasia candida* a sweet wine from Crete, to the island. Its production attracted the taste of connoisseurs from abroad and the fame of the Malvasia, or Malmsey wine, soon spread through the courts of Europe. In 1478 Christopher Columbus visited Madeira to buy sugar; later he returned and married one of the daughters of Bartolomeu, Governor of Porto Santo (see chapter fourteen).

Because of its wide and sheltered position, the bay of Funchal became a natural headquarters for Zarco's administration. It is said that its name derives from *funcho,* the fennel plant found growing in the area. By 1508 Funchal was a city with 5,000 citizens, the archipelago having a general population of 20,000, a tenth of which were slaves. In 1514 Pope Leo X created a bishopric at Madeira.

In 1566 the islands' peace was shattered by the arrival of French pirates commanded by Bertrand de Montluc who raided Funchal, causing great damage to people and property, and to the recently built cathedral. Fourteen years later King Philip II of Spain marched into Portugal, thereby beginning an occupation that was to last sixty years, and which included dominance over the islands of Madeira and Porto Santo. It is interesting to note that many of the ships that formed the Spanish Armada sent to attack England were built from the giant *tils* and *vinhaticos* timber found on Madeira.

The seventeenth and eighteenth centuries

In 1640 the Portuguese finally rose in revolt and expelled their Spanish invaders, the Duke of Braganza being proclaimed King João IV of Portugal, his dominion extending once more to the Madeira archipelago. Twenty years later the marriage of Charles II to Catherine of Braganza strengthened ties between England and

Portugal, leading to a vigorous wine trade between Madeira and English ports and to the establishment of a strong English community on the islands. By 1748 their population had grown to some 75,000 provoking the government to encourage emigration to Brazil by the offer of grants and land to Madeiran couples.

As maritime trade flourished, so many specimens of Madeiran flora were collected and taken to different parts of the world. In 1768 Captain Cook called in with his ship *HMS Endeavour*. The potato was introduced to the islands, and the boats of whalers and tunny-fishers began to call at the ports.

The Napoleonic wars

Towards the end of the eighteenth century the British presence on the island grew as the threat of war with Napoleon became a reality. In 1801 a British garrison was established under the command of Sir William Carr Beresford. Admiral Hood was sent with a fleet carrying 4,000 soldiers, who remained on the islands until 1814, when the threat from France was finally dispelled. The British soldiers proved popular with the local girls, and many married. Some of their modern descendants have fair hair and blue eyes, particularly in Camacha, once a garrison town. These days were also recalled in Santa de Serra, where the drinking fountain once bore the names Taylor, Turner and Hardy.

In August 1815 Napoleon made a brief call for supplies en route to his imprisonment on the island of St Helena. A few years later Madeira's peace was once more disturbed when civil war broke out on the mainland in 1828, a battle for power that raged for six years, when Donna Maria II was finally proclaimed Queen of Portugal.

In 1852 Madeira was struck by plague and famine, and later an outbreak of cholera, that together claimed over 7,000 lives. The failure of the potato crop was accompanied by poor harvests from the sugar plantations, while the islands' vines were struck by the disease *philoxera*. Despite such calamities progress was made in other fields: the first telegraph cable was laid in 1874, linking Madeira direct to Portugal. Rest houses were constructed in the mountains, street lighting illuminated Funchal. In 1891 a young Scotsman by the name of William Reid opened a new luxury hotel on a prominent point overlooking Funchal Harbour, and to this day Reid's Hotel remains one of the most prestigious places to stay on the island.

Into the twentieth century

In 1902 Madeira was granted self-government and eight years later, with the fall of the Portuguese monarchy, it became a part of the Portuguese republic. When the First World War broke out Portugal remained neutral, but in 1916 the Germans declared war, so dragging the nation into the conflict. Madeira did not escape, and the following December Funchal found itself bombarded by German U-boats.

With the peace of 1918 Madeira returned to normality, and continued to develop its agriculture as a main source of income. At the same time an increasing number of visitors came to enjoy the islands' warm climate, and cruise ships began to call regularly. In 1921 the Emperor Charles I of Austria came with his wife to live in Funchal, later moving to Monte.

In 1932 Dr Antonio d'Olivera Salazar became Portugal's Prime Minister, and a year later its virtual dictator. Under his firm rule many reforms were introduced, and he managed to ensure Portuguese neutrality during the Second World War. Madeira did however become a temporary home for over 2,000 evacuees, predominantly women and children, sent by the British Government from Gibraltar in 1943. After the war Churchill paid a visit to Madeira for a holiday in 1949, returning again the following year. He stayed at Reid's Hotel and enjoyed many hours painting at the fishing village of Câmara de Lobos. At that time a seaplane route to Southampton was established, later to be replaced by a landing strip at Porto Santo completed in 1962. Two years later an airport was built on Madeira itself near Santa Cruz, and the growth of tourism on the islands has increased steadily ever since.

In 1968 illness forced Salazar to step down and Dr Marcello Caetano assumed power over Portugal. A time of political upheavel followed, with its own repercussions in Madeira, where intense conflict raged between political parties and their supporters. Many Madeirans suffered hardship: some emigrated, others were deported to South America. The culmination of this unrest was the Popular Revolution of 25th April 1974, when the army overthrew Caetano, a coup that was enthusiastically welcomed by most Madeirans.

In 1976 a constitution was drawn up in Lisbon declaring Madeira and Porto Santo an 'autonomous political region'. This gave the islanders a Regional Government and Parliament, measures that have greatly improved the political structure and living standards of

Madeira. Elections are held every four years, and the majority of seats are presently held by the Popular Social Democratic Party (PDS) led by President Alberto João Jardin. His party is slightly right of centre, and the main opposition is led by the Socialist Party (PS).

Madeira today

Today over 300,000 people live on Madeira, a third of whom reside in its capital Funchal. Walking in the city it is clear that the population is generally healthy and adequately dressed. Only rarely do you see begging. The number of cars in the streets is a good indication that prosperity is on the upward trend.

Out in the country agriculture is still a dominant source of income, but with the increasing number of tourists arriving each year many Madeirans are leaving their farms to work in the hotels and related businesses. A large number of the islanders still emigrate, primarily to South America — there are now some 190,000 Madeirans resident in Venezuela. Others go to Jersey for the hotel season where they are renowned for being hard workers, and many are regularly employed at the same place year after year.

The Madeiran people have a quiet and courteous nature, they are gentle and lead an unhurried life. They have taken to the advent of tourism on their island with tolerance and little anxiety. Over the years Madeira has developed a reputation for its hospitality, and its hotels often cater for the more independent and discerning type of traveller. Since Portugal joined the EEC in 1986 living standards have continued to rise, and the Regional Government is working with other European countries to improve facilities and communications on the islands.

The Madeiran way of life

The Madeirans are a hard-working, tenacious people. Travelling around their islands you cannot fail to be impressed by the large number of farms and smallholdings that have been created out of a very difficult and mountainous terrain. In every deep valley the landscape is dotted with small homesteads clinging perilously to the steep hillsides. Terrace upon terrace has been carved out for cultivation, and even today these are still ploughed by hand, the steepness of the land preventing the use of machinery. Retaining

A weekly occurrence at the port of Funchal — the weighing of a blue marlin.

walls of stone and basalt rocks have been laboriously constructed and maintained in order to keep hold of the precious soil.

In order to irrigate this land the Madeirans have patiently built over the last five hundred years an extensive network of narrow watercourses known as *levadas*. Originally the responsibility of individual farmers, the *levadas* are now under government control, and the modern network stretches some 2,150kms over the land, of which over 40kms runs through tunnels. Often winding along mountainsides and through thickly wooded slopes, these channels make an excellent means of seeing the countryside on account of the narrow concrete paths running alongside them. The local tourist office, the Direccao Regional de Tourismo, encourage visitors to enjoy the benefits of these man-made paths beside the *levadas* (see chapter seven, on Walking).

On the farms you will rarely catch sight of cattle, as all these animals have to be kept inside in small thatched sheds, there being little available pasture. It is only on the high plateau of Pául de Serra that a few sheep and goats can be seen grazing. Towards the south of the island and nearer to sea level, the slopes are covered with vines, and, below these, vast plantations of banana line the

This unusual picture is a common sight in Madeira where young canes are left out to dry prior to basket-weaving.

coast, their large leaves forming a waving green carpet stirred by the Atlantic winds. Along these shores small fishing villages provide a living for sturdy sailors whose brightly painted handbuilt boats make a colourful sight in the day, but which at night are put to sea to work the turbulent waters pounding the rocky shoreline.

Driving through the towns and villages your eyes are constantly drawn to the picturesque countryside, its colour enhanced by the efforts of the locals who love to see bright flowers and shrubs around their property. Every patio, window box, doorstep — even the rooftops — all have tubs and flowerpots that display a mass of blossom and exude sweet aromas. Amidst this blaze of colour you often see an old grandmother, dressed entirely in black, keeping watch over her grandchildren at play. Usually her gnarled fingers will be busy doing the exquisite lacework for which Madeira is so famous.

The Madeirans are a family-loving people with strong ties within their community and with their many distant relations abroad. To the foreign visitor their manner appears quiet and reserved, but it only requires a smile and a 'Bom dia' — 'Good morning' — and instantly their response will be friendly and forthcoming.

Language

The Madeirans speak Portuguese but include their own local dialect. Portuguese is said to be a beautiful and poetic language derived from Latin. Despite that it sounds like an eastern European language when spoken, although it is very similar to Spanish when written. The Madeirans use a sign language which was probably useful to their type of terrain, signalling to each other across gorges, cliffs and mountains.

Fortunately for the tourist, English is widely spoken and it can be said that few problems arise through not being able to speak Portuguese. A Portuguese/English vocabulary of the more common words likely to be encountered is given at Appendix A.

Music and dancing

In spite of this modern age with radio, television and pop music, the Madeirans' natural love of folk music and dancing is evident in the country villages, especially at fiestas and *romarias* (church processions). Children learn these traditions at an early age. Dancing and singing the popular folkloric songs has now become an important tourist attraction in hotels and restaurants.

A number of these dances are of Moorish origin, reflecting the times when slaves from Africa were used by the early settlers. One, called the Dance of the Ponta do Sol, clearly depicts the dejected slow steps of the chained slaves. Another dance has the name of The Heavy Dance because it displays the heavy tread of the workers crushing grapes with their feet. A more cheerful rhythm is The Carriers Dance; it symbolises farm workers heavily laden with loads on their backs jogging along in rhythm to their singing.

A popular dance with tourists is The Handkerchief Dance, where a pretty girl or handsome boy invites a holidaymaker into the dance circle by putting a large colourful handkerchief round their neck, it is great fun and ends with a kiss on both cheeks. The mandolin and the viola *(rajao)* are commonly used, also the accordion. Unique to the island is the *machete,* a guitar-like stringed instrument which is plucked in a steady beat. Sometimes a drum and triangle set the rhythm. But the most unusual instrument of all is the *brinquinho.*

The Madeiran people enjoy folk-dancing as much as the tourists do.

This attractive and colourful instrument is constructed to look like a small hand-held maypole, with tiny costumed dolls attached. The dolls dance up and down, and castanets and bells on their backs make a percussion beat. Hand-clapping and finger-snapping sometimes accompany the dances. Singing is often high pitched and loud.

The traditional Portuguese *fado* songs are sometimes performed as an entertainment in bars, restaurants and hotels. Of Arabic origin, the songs are often sad, telling stories of human life, tragedy, love, hate and jealousy, *Fado* means fate. Usually the singer is a woman with a powerful voice who is accompanied by a guitar and sometimes a mandolin or zither.

The costumes worn by singers and dancers vary from village to village. You can have your first sight of these colourful clothes in Funchal for in 1933 it was decreed that all flowersellers in Funchal market must wear the attractive national costume. There you can see women wearing wide multicoloured vertical striped skirts, the predominant colours being red, orange and black with a band at the hem. A white blouse is often beautifully embroidered or adorned with hand-made lace, the sleeves are elbow length. A tight-fitting coloured waistcoat is worn, sometimes covered by a red woollen cape slung over one shoulder. Both men and women wear traditional boots, called *botachá,* (literally 'plain boot'). They are made of tanned goat-skin, ox-hide or calf-skin, and are knee length but rolled down round the ankle. To complete the woman's outfit there is the *carapuca,* a small blue cap with red trimming and a small stalk in the middle. The man's costume consists of a white suit with red cummerbund and black waistcoat with a colourful kerchief tied round the neck. Sometimes men wear a traditional wool hat, the *barreye de la,* similar to a familiar bobble cap, with ear flaps that can be worn up or down. In the countryside these are usually hand knitted in dark brown or cream colour wool. Nowadays these hats are sold as souvenirs at around 2,300 escudos (£10).

Folklore

Madeira has many traditions which go back to the early days of settlement on the island. A good example is the Slaughtering of the Pig, which is done at the Christmas season, starting in early December. At the beginning of each new year young piglets are bought and fattened throughout the year for the yuletide celebrations. At the time of slaughter there are family celebrations with much bustle around the pigsty. The hog is always killed with a very sharp knife so that the animal suffers as little as possible. The animal's blood is collected and used to make tasty dishes. Then the pig is singed over a bonfire and the innards removed; next day it is cut up and wrapped in clean cloths, part is pickled while the rest is divided amongst the family. This is a deep rooted festivity and a time when melodic traditional songs are sung and much wine is drunk.

Handicrafts

Over the years the men and women of Madeira have become very dexterous. Of necessity they have had to be good boat builders and to this day, when you visit Machico, you are likely to see a wooden craft on the stocks in the little shipyard.

Eleven kilometres from Funchal the village of Camacha is the centre of the wicker-work industry, where tourists can visit a factory and see some of the processes and skills of making wicker-work. Note that no wires, glue or nails are used to fashion the items. Over two thousand craftsmen and women are employed to weave the willow cane into a vast selection of baskets, furniture and other useful household items. The willow which is grown in the damp valleys is never allowed to grow tall, being cut between January and March; it is then soaked in water, peeled and dried but left sufficiently supple to allow it to be weaved. It is a familiar sight on the island to see bunches of willow rods on roof tops or stacked beside cottages, for as well as the factories this is very much a cottage industry. It goes back to the time when it was work for the winter when the land was too wet to cultivate. Today wicker-work is still an important export industry.

It was back in 1850 that an English woman, Miss Elizabeth Phelps, the daughter of a wine importer, noticed the fine stitchwork done by the Madeiran women in their spare time. She took some of this work to show her friends in London who immediately asked her to take orders for some of the exquisite embroidery. In time this Madeiran fine art embroidery became a thriving business. Now it is one of the island's major activities employing over twenty thousand women.

Madeira's tapestry work, though not so well known, is claimed to be an even older skill with the authorities issuing a decree to

The hand carved whales will soon become rare.

support the craft in 1780; and tapestries were on display at the Madeiran International Fair in 1850. Chair covers, cushions, handbags and wall hangings are worked in delicate petit point. Subjects range from the beautiful flowers of Madeira to famous Flemish paintings.

There is a governing body, the Instituto do Bordado Tapecarias e Artesanato de Madeira, which supervises the industry of the island's handicrafts of embroidery, tapestry and wicker-work. All embroideries are inspected and sealed, in order to maintain a high standard of work and guarantee the authenticity of the art.

Other industry on the island includes pottery, ceramics, straw hats, wooden ornaments, costume dolls and edible commodities.

Public holidays and festivals

During the year there are quite a number of events taking place, so you may like to time your visit to Madeira to attend some occasion of interest to you. The exact dates of some of these celebrations can change, but the tourist office in London should be able to provide you with an up-to-date calendar of events. Contact the Portuguese National Tourist Office, 1-5 New Bond Street, London W1Y 0NP. Tel: 01 493 3873.

An important event in February is Funchal's carnival starting on Shrove Tuesday. Also in this month are family festivities in the village of Santana on the north coast, with processions and fireworks. April provides a flower festival, June an eight-day musical festival, held in the Municipal Theatre and the Sé Cathedral in Funchal. Also in June is a sheep shearing festival, where the women do the shearing and there is much eating, drinking and dancing. In August the Madeira wine rally and championship is held, which has the backing of the national and European Automobile Association. This two-day event car rally is quite famous, with participants from all parts of the world, and the rally route covers the whole island. On the last Sunday in August, Machico celebrates the festival of the Holy Sacrament. Also in Machico during September there are great bonfires in the mountains for the Saint Silvester Sacrament Festival, and processions for Our Lord of Milagres take place on 8 and 9 October.

Remember that on public holidays, shops, offices and banks will be closed although a few shops may be open in tourist areas and certainly most cafés and restaurants. Bus services are likely to be curtailed and petrol service stations closed. Shops, offices and banks may also close on 24 and 26 December. Up-to-date information will be provided by the Tourist Office, Avenida Arriaga 18, Funchal. Tel: 29057. Hotel receptions should also have some information.

Public Holidays in Madeira

January	1	New Year's Day
Movable		Shrove Tuesday
Movable		Good Friday
April	25	Day of Revolution
May	1	Worker's Day
Movable		Corpus Christi
June	10	Portuguese National Day
July	1	Regional Day
August	15	Feast of the Assumption
August	21	Funchal Day
October	5	Republic Day
November	1	All Saints' Day
December	1	Independence Day
December	8	The Immaculate Conception
December	25	Christmas Day
December	31	Saint Silvester

Island flora

Perhaps the subject that people talk about most when Madeira is mentioned is the abundance of natural vegetation and colourful flora found on the island. This is why the phrase 'Floating Garden' is often used to describe the Madeiran countryside. We can only give here a general picture of what can be admired during a short holiday. Over the past years a number of specialist books have been written about Madeira's landscapes and countryside, where you can find detailed descriptions and colourful illustrations.

Thanks to its situation, geography and mild climate, Madeira has atmospheric conditions which are just about ideal for the growth of most plants. The misty clouds and high humidity, together with warm sunshine, create a gardener's paradise. A visit to the Botanical Gardens and the Quinta do Palheiro will enable you to see almost at a glance the wonderful array of exotic trees, plants and flowers which flourish here.

You will be amazed how quickly the scenery can change with the altitude and situation. A drive up into the mountain zone between six hundred and thirteen hundred metres brings you into magnificent forests where, on the southern slopes, the typical laurels grow. *Ocotea foetes,* the till tree or stink laurel and the *persea indica,* the vinhatico (related to the mimosa), are evergreen. These sturdy tall trees were once in demand for building ships: both are now used to make furniture. Other trees in this higher ground are the shiny laurel *(laurus azorical),* and two hollies *(ilex perado* and *ilex canariensis).* The tree shrubs of *erica arborea* and *erica scoparia* are heathers that will reach a height of three metres; it is an unusual sight if you have previously seen only low heather growing on the hills and moorlands of Great Britain. Other trees amongst the forestal regions have been introduced by former settlers, to be grown for economic reasons, they include the oak, the fragrant pine, the eucalyptus and the acacia. In the same area you will probably see the the Madeiran bilberry *(vaccinium Maderense)* growing. This edible fruit is about a centimetre in diameter. In some parts of the island bilberries are cultivated for export.

Exotic flowers, cactus and shrubs are to be seen in every garden.

In the humid atmosphere of the laurel woods the small Madeira orchid *(dactylorhiza foliosa)* grows at an altitude of between six hundred and a thousand metres. Its flowers are a rosy purple on a thin spike with shiny green lanceolate leaves. They bloom from May to July. This orchid is not found in any other part of the world. There are five indigenous species of orchid in Madeira, three of them endemic. The Cymbidium orchid is now cultivated in vast quantities (some for export) between the months of February and the end of May. Cymbidium can be white, yellowish green, rose coloured and brown speckled; the stalks have eight to ten blooms and are about twelve centimetres in diameter, and they have spikes of about one metre or more. This most spectacular of flowers is seen in giant floral arrangements in many of the hotels and can be purchased in flower shops and at the airport.

Back in the countryside and lower down the mountains by the coastal zones, trees, shrubs and many herbs thrive. The edible purple passion fruit *(passiflora edulis)* does well from sea level up to five hundred metres. The *agave Americana* is a succulent plant common in arid terrain, as are the *aloes, arborescens* and *aloe Plicatilis,* whose giant orange floral spikes may be one metre high. Originally from South Africa they are acclimatised now to Madeira.

Mention must be made of the enormous variety of aromatic herbs, grasses and wild ferns, like the ivy leaf fern *(asplenium)* and the liver wort *(adiantum reniforme).* The Madeiran vipers bugloss *(echium candicans)* also called the Pride of Madeira blooms from May to July. The tall spiky flowers are a purple shade of blue and are endemic.

In villages and towns yet more colourful trees, shrubs, flowers and pot plants brighten the landscape. Walls are covered with wisteria, bignonias, honeysuckle and bougainvillea. One of the prime sights in Funchal, if you are there between April and June, is the jacaranda tree-lined streets, which are a haze of mauve blue flowers.

Whichever time of the year you visit Madeira you can be sure of finding a floral bouquet:

- **January** Orchids are everywhere, and many coloured bougainvillea and the scented mimosa.
- **February** The coral tree has deep red flowers which bloom at the end of each branch. The majestic camellia's creamy petals seem to be made of wax.
- **March** Azaleas spread their varied hues, the jasmine and delicate wisteria their perfumes.

Funchal at Fiesta time. Note the beautiful jacaranda trees in bloom during May.

- **April** The purple jacaranda blossoms along the Avenida Arriaga in Funchal. Agapanthus, seen growing wild on the countryside verges, open their petals of blue or white flowers.
- **May** Now the honeysuckle spreads a sweet trail, the lupins and anthuriums make a bright display.
- **June** All is a riot of blossom in this warm sunshine. See the Pride of Madeira, the large-headed hydrangea and the mighty magnolia trees in bloom.
- **July** The glorious hibiscus sheds its coloured petals and the ornamental *tipana tipu* tree drops its yellow flowers too, making a carpet of gold everywhere.
- **August** The deep wine red amaranthus stands straight and tall as does the *Yucca Gloriosa,* with its tulip-like creamy white flowering stem. Look for the cheerful oleander, too, a sign of warm days.
- **September** Time for belladonna lilies to spread over the waste ground and gardens with their attractive trumpet shaped blooms, offering a sweet perfume that rivals the frangipani tree for fragrance.

- **October** Climbing over walls and trellis the allamanda only shows its soft yellow blooms along the southern coast. Also clinging is the strawberry pear *(hylocerus undatus)* whose attractive green, white and yellow flower opens at night.
- **November** Wintertime is when to admire the floss silk tree, *(chorisia speciosa)* with its lovely rose-coloured floral display. Of a similar shade is the low growing *oxalis purporea.*
- **December** Among the glittering decorations and luminous streets, the trees and flowers of Madeira still glow. Heralding the coming of Christmas are the deep red bracts of the poinsettia and the yellow-scented flowers of the silver wattle trees.

To complete the miscellany of Madeira's garden, perhaps the most striking of all the plants and the one that grows all the year is the *strelitzia reginae.* This highly admired plant, looking so important and amazingly similar to an exotic bird, is familiarly called the Bird of Paradise flower. It rates high in the export market because as a cut flower it will last for about three weeks.

This bouquet of Madeira's best-known flowers includes the unusual Bird of Paradise flower and orchids.

Wild life

Madeira is a very safe island because there are no ferocious wild animals or reptiles, only the friendly frog and the lizard *(lacerta dugessi)* which the Portuguese call Lagartixa. These lizards, some of which can be as large as seventeen centimetres in length and one and a half centimetres round the body, are fascinating. In varying colours of black and greeny brown they are seen darting along walls and in between the rocks, especially when the sun is shining. But you will have to be very quick, quiet and still if you wish to photograph or observe them for at the slightest noise or movement they slip out of sight. The farmers do not like them because they eat the fruits, especially the grapes.

There are a few 'nasties' in the insect world. You may encounter mosquitoes, which breed in water tanks and wells and can be a nuisance on a tender skin. There are lots of beetles, too, but harmless ones and mostly they keep out of sight, except for the unwelcome cockroach. Flies and bluebottles are about all the year. Ants can be a bother; it is said that there are about ten different species. Watch out for spiders, reputedly a hundred different types nearly all harmless, but be careful of a large black spider, the *lycosa trachosa blackwalli,* whose bite can cause discomfort. *Epeira aurelia* is the Madeiran tarantula which is striped with black and silver. On the uninhabited island of Deserta Grande is the biggest spider of all, the *lycosa trachosa igens,* black and poisonous with a bite that can be fatal. However you are most unlikely to come across any of these!

More pleasant creatures abound, such as moths and butterflies of which there are about one hundred and twenty different species, many being particularly colourful. Various snails are to be found only on the islands: one hundred and thirty-one species, sixty-one found on Madeira, forty-four on Porto Santo, ten located on the Desertas, and the remaining sixteen that are common to all the islands. Periwinkles, limpets and whelks are found along the sea shores and some small crabs but few edible lobsters.

The rabbit was once introduced to Porto Santo by its first Governor Perestreto and together with rats they are found in large numbers on both islands.

Birds

Numerous sea birds can be observed around the Madeiran archipelago, the high cliffs making an ideal nesting place for the birds that breed here. The list is long but the more familiar are the storm petrel, Manx shearwater, common tern and Atlantic herring gull. On land you may sight eagles, kestrels, sparrow hawks, buzzards, partridge, woodcock, quails, owls, swifts, warblers, finches, wagtails, blackbirds and sparrows, to name but a few of the forty-two species that breed on the islands. Sometimes migratory birds are swept here by the east wind that comes from the African coast.

The Portuguese Government has bought the Selvagen Islands with their one hundred metre high cliffs and declared them a bird sanctuary, and so now they are guarded. The nearer Deserta Islands are bird sanctuaries too, and occasionally seals can be seen by the caves.

Fish

The clear blue waters around Madeira abound in fish and marine vegetation. Whales, dolphins, porpoises and seals may sometimes be spotted. Sea bream, perch, grey mullet, moray and conger eel can be fished by the angler from the jetty in Funchal harbour. Further out in deep waters some two hundred and fifty species of fish have been recorded. Amongst the very big ones are sharks, tuna, swordfish and marlin. Edible fish also include mackerel and sardines.

Something really different is the *espada,* also called a scabbard fish, which is almost unique to Madeiran waters. It is a shiny black fish, long and narrow with spines along its back, and a large vicious mouth and glaring eyes. It is about a metre long, weighing between one and two kilos. It has some resemblance to an eel. This is the fish that is always on the menu in Madeira's fish restaurants. Despite its horrid appearance, when cooked it makes a most delicious and delicate tasting meal. The *espada* is caught only at night, to prevent other fish from devouring them before the catch is brought to the surface. They lie in very deep waters so no one really knows their life habits. Jacques Cousteau once tried to trace where they bred, but even with his sophisticated equipment he was unable to descend deep enough to make the study. Because the *espada* lives at such depth, when it is caught by the fishermen and brought quickly to the surface it dies from decompression. In fact it is probable that no one has ever seen this fish alive. But you will see plenty of these fish for sale if you can get to Funchal's fish market early in the morning.

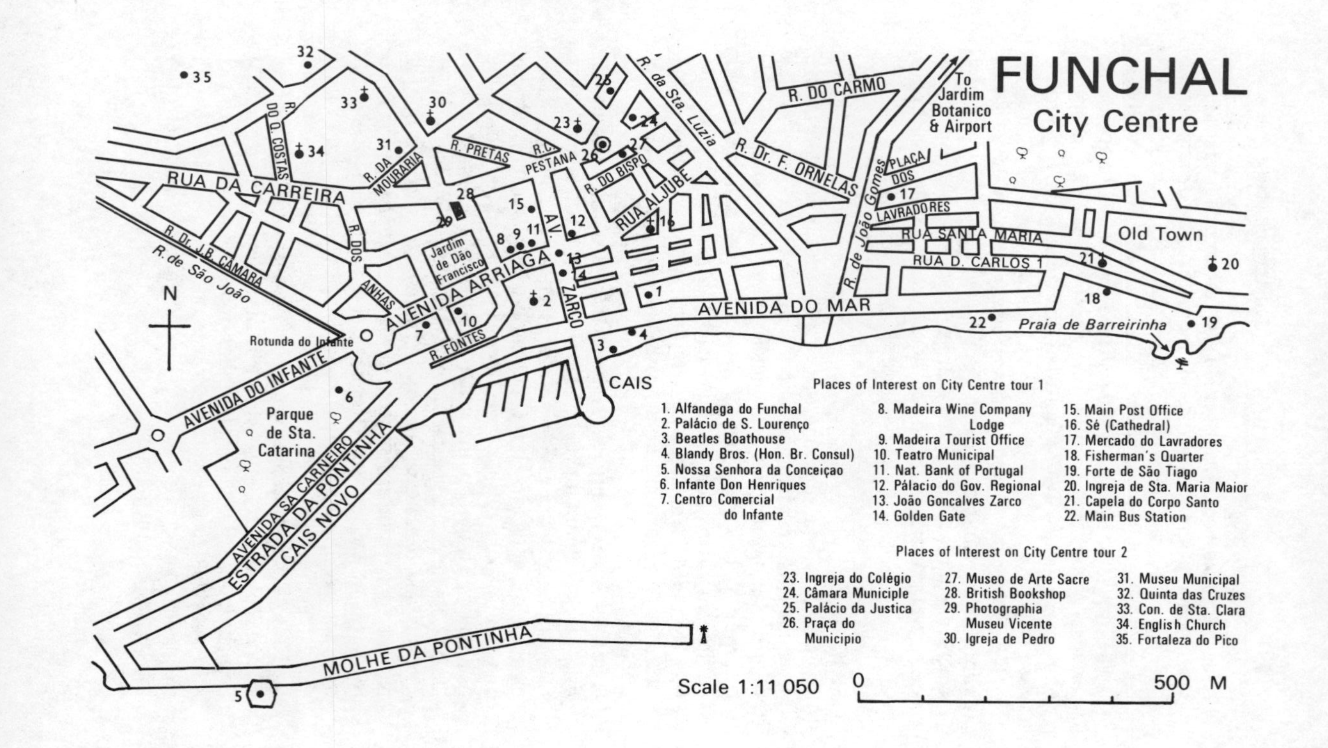
FUNCHAL
City Centre
To Jardim Botanico & Airport
R. DO CARMO
R. da Sta. Luzia
R. Dr. F. ORNELAS
R. de João Gomes
PLAÇA DOS LAVRADORES
RUA SANTA MARIA
RUA D. CARLOS 1
Old Town
AVENIDA DO MAR
Praia de Barreirinha
RUA DA CARREIRA
R. DO Q. COSTAS
R. DA MOURARIA
R. PRETAS
R. C. PESTANA
R. DO BISPO
RUA ALJUBE
AV. ZARCO
AVENIDA ARRIAGA
Jardim de Dão Francisco
R. DOS ANHAS
R. Dr. J.B. CAMARA
R. de São João
N
Rotunda do Infante
R. FONTES
AVENIDA DO INFANTE
Parque de Sta. Catarina
AVENIDA SA CARNEIRO
ESTRADA DA PONTINHA
CAIS NOVO
CAIS
MOLHE DA PONTINHA
Places of Interest on City Centre tour 1
1. Alfandega do Funchal
2. Palácio de S. Lourenço
3. Beatles Boathouse
4. Blandy Bros. (Hon. Br. Consul)
5. Nossa Senhora da Conceiçao
6. Infante Don Henriques
7. Centro Comercial do Infante
8. Madeira Wine Company Lodge
9. Madeira Tourist Office
10. Teatro Municipal
11. Nat. Bank of Portugal
12. Pálacio do Gov. Regional
13. João Goncalves Zarco
14. Golden Gate
15. Main Post Office
16. Sé (Cathedral)
17. Mercado do Lavradores
18. Fisherman's Quarter
19. Forte de São Tiago
20. Ingreja de Sta. Maria Maior
21. Capela do Corpo Santo
22. Main Bus Station
Places of Interest on City Centre tour 2
23. Ingreja do Colégio
24. Câmara Municiple
25. Palácio da Justica
26. Praça do Municipio
27. Museo de Arte Sacre
28. British Bookshop
29. Photographia Museu Vicente
30. Igreja de Pedro
31. Museu Municipal
32. Quinta das Cruzes
33. Con. de Sta. Clara
34. English Church
35. Fortaleza do Pico
Scale 1:11 050
0
500 M

NINE

Funchal

The capital of Madeira is situated in a bay on the southern coast. The city is built around the harbour, spreading out like a fan up the steep sides of the mountains that lie behind the buildings. Four rivers cut through the city. In the west is Ribeira Seco, quite near Reid's Hotel. Next come Ribeira de São João and then Ribeiras de Santa Luzia and de João Gomes; these last two are almost hidden by trailing colourful bougainvillea and are dry for most of the year.

History

It was João Goncalves Zarco, one of the explorers who discovered Madeira, who first founded Funchal. The name derives from the vast quantity of fennel *(funcho)* that grew in the city — alas, no longer to be seen. Zarco was appointed Governor of this area and he drew the plans for the city, settled here with his family, and ruled for forty years. In 1508, King Manuel of Portugal granted a charter to Funchal, which had prospered from its sugar trade, and the city took as its crest four sugar loaves.

The original centre of the city was marked in the west by the Fort of São Tiago (Saint James) and to the west by Fort São Lourenço (Saint Lawrence), with most buildings clustering round the Cathedral and the left bank of the River João Gomes. As Funchal became more of a commercial city it expanded to the right bank of the river in the Santa Maria district.

It is said that the oldest constructed road in Funchal is Santa Maria Road which runs parallel to the sea. Typical styles of architecture used for the buildings in Rua Santa Maria can still be seen today, as this area is protected by legislation. During the seventeenth and eighteenth centuries many fine estates *(quintas)* were established on the outskirts of the city by successful businessmen.

the nineteenth century sailing and steam ships used Funchal rbour on their way to South Africa and the Americas. Private yachts, carrying important persons and sometimes royalty, also called. Later on luxury liners made Funchal a port of call. But since the opening of airports on Porto Santo and Madeira the harbour is now mainly used by cargo and fishing boats. However, Funchal is not short of visitors who come in from their apartments and hotels by car, bus and taxi.

The capital today

A distant view of Funchal today presents an attractive picture of many red roofed buildings and tall church spires, intermingled with luxuriant greenery. Only a closer look reveals the bustle, noise and the unfortunate pollution from the many cars, buses and trucks. Funchal now suffers from a traffic problem, which hopefully will soon be relieved when the new ring road is completed.

Over a third of Madeira's population live in Funchal, and many more enter the city daily for work, so parking is difficult. However, there is an excellent bus service serving the whole of the island from Funchal and plenty of good taxis to take you to and from the city. And you can take a coach tour of the city itself.

Here you will find an abundance of cafés, restaurants and small shops. Modern shopping arcades mean that you have a large selection under one roof. The Tourist Office is easily located at Avenida Arriaga 18 and will provide maps of the city and the island, taxi tour charges, information on hotels and much more free information. For a small fee you can have a bus timetable.

Funchal, despite the traffic, is a delightful city to explore on foot and not too large. The main tourist attractions can be seen in one full day, but better to allow two if possible, and longer if you like to linger in museums and churches. Be sure to wear suitable footwear because some of the streets are cobbled with smooth round stones that are slippery and uneven. In the centre, footpaths have small black and white stones in a mosaic pattern which is attractive. Remember to take your camera, for many of the older buildings have ornate stone and wrought ironwork. Most of the town houses have charming gardens with graceful courtyards, containing flowers and potted plants and ferns. The traditional colours of the buildings are cream walls, pale grey paint work and green shutters and doors; roofs have red tiles. All this is now required by legislation.

This aerial view of Funchal harbour shows clearly the old fortress of Nossa Senhora da Conceição and the tunnel leading to the new quay.

City centre tour 1

If you arrive in Funchal by taxi you are more than likely to find yourself close to the Cathedral, where the city's main taxi rank is located. Coming here by bus or coach you will probably alight along the seafront on the Avenida do Mar (also called Avenida das Communidades Madeirenses). Should you arrive by car, try parking near the main bus station at the eastern end of the Avenida do Mar (but we do not guarantee you a space!).

Funchal has a long waterfront, and it is very pleasant to start your tour of the city by walking along this seafront. The promenade is wide with gardens and seats, the road a dual carriageway. From here there is a pleasant view of the city which stretches northwards, up the hills into the mountains. You will be amazed at the steepness of some of the narrow cobbled streets.

Along the waterfront, blocks of five-storey offices and shops line the inland side of the Avenida do Mar, until you reach the sixteenth-century **Alfandega do Funchal** (Customs House) and **Palácio de Sâo Lourenço** (Palace of Saint Lawrence), a large white edifice with many windows and turreted corners. Although a palace, it was once an important fortification and is now a Portuguese national monument. It is also the residence of Madeira's military governor and is guarded by sentries with modern automatic weapons, but some of the historic cannons can still be seen. It is not open to the public.

On the seaside is the **Cais,** the old quay, which has steps leading down to the modern yacht marina. It is a picturesque sight to see the different types of leisure craft moored here. Nearby are the marine offices and information for booking a ticket on the catamaran *Independencia,* which ferries daily between Madeira and the tiny island of Porto Santo. Floral gardens near the marina and a restaurant makes this a popular place for all to meet and relax. An unusual sight is the **Beatles Boathouse,** now part of another open air restaurant complex. Yes, it did once belong to that pop group. Opposite the Beatles Boathouse is the office of the Honorary British Consul, which is in the building of **Blandy Brothers,** travel agents.

An unusual landmark, the Beatles boat is now beached forever.

Continuing our walk westwards, past some old fashioned kiosks selling drinks, sweets and cigarettes, we see below on the shore the building of the busy new fish market and installations for the fishing boats. Now we are by the **Cais Nova,** the new quay. The road is called Estrada da Pontinha. The breakwater, Molhe da Pontinha, was built at the end of the eighteenth century and later a hole was bored in a rocky islet called Loo Rock, to allow the quay to be much extended. It is here that cruise liners now berth. There are toilets along here, but they are not always open. You may care to look at the old fortress of **Nossa Senhora da Conceiçao** and on reaching the end of the breakwater you will have a good panoramic view of Funchal.

Back on the Estrada da Pontinha you will notice on the inland side of the road some beautiful gardens, overlooking the harbour. It is the **Parque de Santa Catarina.** At the end of this road be careful of traffic, for it is a very busy junction and roundabout, the **Rotunda do Infante.** In the centre is a large fountain that looks very pretty at night when it is floodlit. At the bottom of the Santa Catarina park is a large statue of Infante Don Henriques (Prince Henry the Navigator).

We now go three quarters of the way (clockwise) round the roundabout and find ourselves in Avenida Arriaga. This is one of the busiest streets in Funchal and is a dual carriageway but it can be a sheer delight to the eye if you are in Madeira during May and June. Then the whole avenue is lined with a soft haze of mauve blossom, from the spreading jacaranda trees, a wonderful sight.

Now you will see on the sea side of this avenue the high modern block of the **Centro Comercial do Infante,** always busy and noisy with pop music seven days a week. It contains a great variety of shops, bars, restaurants and supermarkets on three levels, with offices and apartments on the floor above.

Opposite here are the public gardens called **Jardim de São Francisco** which are a restful haven for weary sightseers. Close to the pavement is a fountain in a pool with a trickling waterfall. Graceful black swans and friendly ducks glide around a joyful statue of two little boys at play, which is especially cheerful when illuminated. This is a place where you can sit on a bench and have your shoes shined, or your photograph taken, and just relax in the sunshine amongst the bright flowers and tropical trees. Here you can observe how the citizens of Funchal go about their daily lives. A quiet people who are always polite, they will do their best to help you when you need assistance or directions to a place. Amongst the brilliant flower beds, shrubs and cobbled paths in this botanical garden is a statue of Saint Francis, while at a higher level are a bandstand and auditorium.

A little further along the avenue and on the same side as the gardens, you come to the **Madeira Wine Company Lodge** with a museum and wine-tasting rooms. It is open to the public who are welcome to make purchases. Next door is the Secretaria Regional do Turismo e Cultura at number 18 — the **Madeira Tourist Office.** Do take advantage of the facilities offered. The receptionists are charmingly helpful and speak English. Maps of island and city are given willingly. They also have a selection of guide books about Madeira that you can purchase.

Across the avenue on the southern side is the **Teatro Municiple,** the municipal theatre, opened in 1888. The little auditorium has three tiers rising vertically. It was restored in the 1970s and is used now as a theatre, concert hall and cinema. Next door is a fine old Madeiran house which has, on its outside walls, *azulejos* (blue and white tiles) showing lively scenes that depict the olden way of life in Madeira. Inside it is a modern car sales room. How things change!

Now we have reached an important road junction, where Avenida Zarco crosses from north to south the Avenida Arriaga. On the northern corners are huge imposing buildings, to the west is the **National Bank of Portugal** and to the east, the **Pálacio do Governo Regional,** which is the island's regional administrative headquarters, a lovely building with many windows, a coat of arms on the wall and attractive patios.

On the central reservation of these cross roads, on a tall plinth, is a large statue of **João Goncalves Zarco** by the Madeiran sculptor Francisco Franco. South of this statue is what is known as the **Golden Gate,** for here are pavement cafés where you can sit in the sunshine and meet people from all over the world. To reach the **main post office** you must turn north up Avenida Zarco and it is on the left. Inside it is modern and large and offers the usual postal services; here you can send a telex and make an international telephone call.

Back by Zarco's statue (it is a useful place to meet friends) you will see towards the east the great **Sé,** Madeira's cathedral, built by the Knights of the Order of Christ in the fifteenth century. It was the first Portuguese cathedral to be erected overseas. From this view the cathedral appears to be small for much of the main building lies behind the simple frontage. It is constructed of white stucco and black volcanic basalt, with reddish tufa rock. The portal in Gothic style has an arch with the royal Portuguese arms at its peak. High

Surely this is the most appealing sight in Avenida Arriaga, especially when the fountain plays.

above is a rose window. The tall square belfry tower is crenellated and above the clock face is a pointed dark blue and white tiled steeple.

Inside the dark interior of the cathedral may come as a surprise, after the bright sunshine outside. But sit awhile; the candlelight and people at prayer will bring a sense of calm and you will feel refreshed. High above is the original Moorish ceiling of cedar wood and ivory in Mudejar style. The nave, with its graceful columns, has three aisles, and the choir stalls are delicately carved in cedar wood. The acoustics are very good and orchestral concerts are performed here. By the altar are Portuguese paintings of medieval scenes. The sixteenth-century Sacramento Chapel is to the right of the chancel, richly Baroque in its marble and gilded wood. Part of the cathedral's treasures are guarded in the Museu de Arte Sacre (see chapter seven).

Outside again we continue our walk eastwards, now along the Rua Aljube. On the cathedral side of the road sit a group of colourful **flowersellers.** Huge sprays of orchids. Birds of Paradise flowers, sweetly perfumed carnations and many other varieties tempt the passerby. The Madeirans are very fond of flowers, both in their gardens and houses.

On the other side of the road are smart expensive shops, jewellers, silversmiths and boutiques. Should you buy a garment, any alterations necessary will be completed within a few hours, as tailors are always available to give a quick service. There are plenty of shoe shops, too. Should your size be out of stock it is likely that the owner will send along the street to find what you require. Good service and politeness are still very much in evidence in the shops of Funchal. One strange quirk, when you go into a cake shop *(pastelaria),* you need to pay for your choice before you have it wrapped.

Now if you wish you can cross a bridge over one of Funchal's rivers, **Ribeira de Santa Luzia,** then walk down the busy Rua Dr Fernao Ornelas; there are lots of interesting shops here. At the end of this street there is another river to cross, **Ribeira de João Gomes,** but you will hardly realise it is a river as it is covered with a trellis work of lovely purple bougainvillea.

There will be no mistaking the entrance to Funchal's main market in the Plaça dos Lavradores, for in the mornings it is a teeming mass of people with loaded bags and baskets of produce. **Mercado do Lavradores** (the workers market) is an old building with lots of activity and charm. Inside you will first see a mass of colour from the flowersellers in folk costume. Although busy selling and sorting flowers they are very patient about having their photographs taken again and again — even smiling for you. Fruit and vegetable vendors have their produce in large wicker baskets but they do not shout or harass the customers. Hats, handbags and basket stalls mix with egg and cheese products! There is plenty of fresh meat in the market, but do not expect the cuts to be the same as in the UK. If in doubt, why not buy some minced beef *(carne do picado);* half a kilo will be just over a pound in weight.

To our mind the most exciting part of the market is downstairs, where you will find the fish market. Just stand for a moment at the top of the steps and gaze at this splendid scene of activity. Look at the enormous round tuna fish being cut into slices — not for the squeamish, perhaps. Then your eye will be caught by the most predominant fish there, and one you probably have never seen before, the *espada* or scabbard fish. These eel-like black fish are a metre or more in length and lie across the bench; their evil-looking head, with pointed face and protruding eyes, and their spiky gills look really horrible. Yet it is the favourite fish of Madeira and all tourist restaurants serve it in delicious fish dishes.

The Municipal Gardens with their exotic plants make a restful place for everyone.

Funchal's meeting point, the statue of Zarco the Explorer.

Having seen the market you can go seawards and in to the **Old Town.** It is a maze of little streets, many cobbled with shabby houses, but there are some good seafood restaurants and *fado* singing here as you are near the **Fishermen's Quarter,** old fishing harbour. The **Forte de São Tiago** was once used by the British Army garrisoned here in 1801, and is now used by the local military police. Nearby is a stony beach, **Praia de Barreirinha,** with sunbathing terraces and pools for children to use.

While here you will notice the onion-shaped dome of the eighteenth-century church **Ingreja de Santa Maria Maior,** in Largo Sororro; it contains a shrine to Saint James for protecting the Madeirans from a sixteenth-century plague. On 1 May each year this is the scene of a great religious festival. Another older chapel is the **Capela do Corpo Santo,** built by the Guild of Fishermen at the end of the fifteenth century, in honour of the fishermen's patron saint, Saint Peter. It is open to the public.

While in this area you are very close to the **main bus station** down on the Avenida do Mar. It is not a building but just a large parking place for coaches and buses to depart and arrive.

City centre tour 2

As Zarco's statue in the centre of Funchal is so noticeable, we are starting this tour from there. Walk up Avenida Zarco, past the post office and at the top turn right into Rua C. Prestana. You will notice the English Chemist on the corner. Not very far away are three important and imposing buildings, the **Ingreja do Colégio** (Church of Saint John the Evangelist), **Câmara Municiple** (Town Hall), and the **Palácio da Justica** (Law Courts). If you have the Tourist Office's free map of Funchal this will help you identify them. The **Praça do Municipio** (Municipal Square) is wide and very attractive with all these mighty buildings around it. The Collegiate Church was founded in the seventeenth century and built by the Jesuits, its facade is Baroque, with marble statues of saints in niches. The Town Hall once belonged to the second Conde de Carvalhal as a private residence. It has a symmetrical frontage and a pretty tiled patio with flowering trees. A few hundred metres southwards is Rua do Bispo 21, where you find the **Museo de Arte Sacre** (Museum of Sacred Art, see chapter seven). It is another fine building which was once a Bishop's Palace but now contains paintings, sculptures and religious treasures, some of which were in the Sé Cathedral.

It is now necessary to return to the top of Avenida Zarco (by the English Chemist). Walk a few metres along Rua da Carreira and at number 43 you will see the entrance to the **British Bookshop.** Here is the patio leading to **Photographia Museu Vicente.** This patio courtyard has a unique look of old world charm with its potted ferns and faded decor of wrought iron columns and ornate roof valances. Despite the fact that the cobbled ground now has tables and chairs belonging to the café restaurant there, it still retains an air of gentility. The Photographic Museum (see chapter seven) is open only in the afternoon and entrance is free. This old courtyard also has a music shop and a health food shop, which is always busy at lunch time.

On the corner of Rua Pretas is **Igreja de Pedro** (Saint Peter's Church) originally built in 1598 and then restored in 1748. It's a quiet church which few tourists seem to visit. Five minutes away down hill in a narrow cobbled street, at Rua da Mouraria 31, is the **Museu Municipal.** Once an eighteenth-century palace belonging to Conde de Carvalhal, it now houses the regional historic archives and the natural history museum, while downstairs there is a small aquarium containing species of marine life found in the waters around Madeira. It is closed on Mondays. This is a place to bring the children as upstairs there are huge stuffed whales, seals, swordfish, turtles and other creatures one rarely sees. It is a bit eerie down in the aquarium as it is kept dark and some of the fish look fierce but others are quite beautiful. The fish are fed at 1500 hrs.

Continuing our walk we now come to two really lovely buildings, full of interest, both historical and visual. At Calcada do Pico 1, is the **Quinta das Cruzes,** said to have been the site of the home of João Goncalves Zarco. This sturdy house dates from the seventeenth century. It was rebuilt in the nineteenth century and today it is still furnished in that period. Lovers of fine antiques and those interested in the history of Madeira will enjoy walking round this well laid out museum. Each room is varied in its contents, one being devoted entirely to a great collection of antique silver. You can even wander down to the cellars and wine stores. There is a set of beautifully coloured postcards showing the contents of the house and grounds, which can be purchased as a reminder of this eminent museum.

Before you depart do find time to look round the botanical gardens that surround this *quinta,* for they contain surprising treasures, such as two stone Manueline windows and armorial bearings, as well as many trees from all parts of the world, bright floral specimens and a fine orchid house.

This Patio, outside the Photographia Museu Vicente, is worth seeking for refreshments and an interesting museum with old world surroundings.

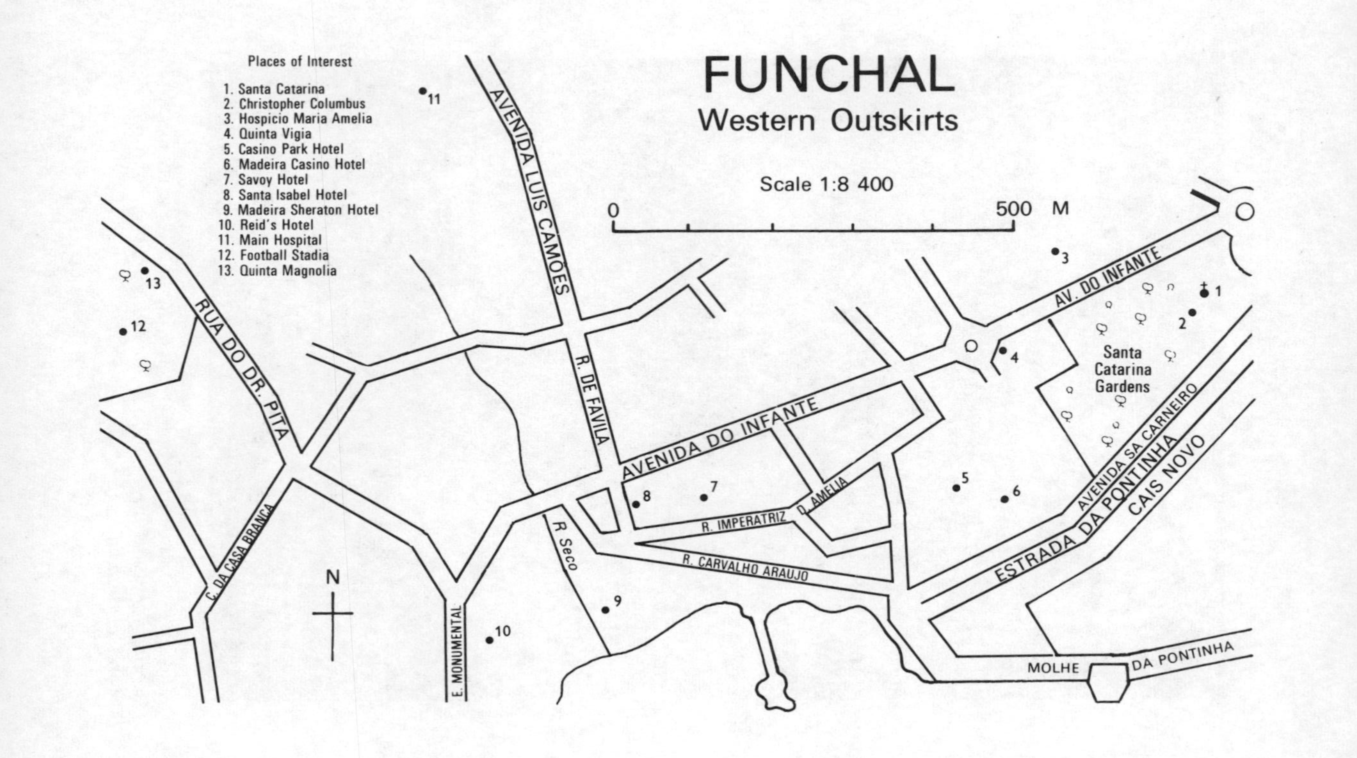
FUNCHAL
Western Outskirts
Scale 1:8 400
0
500 M
Places of Interest
1. Santa Catarina
2. Christopher Columbus
3. Hospicio Maria Amelia
4. Quinta Vigia
5. Casino Park Hotel
6. Madeira Casino Hotel
7. Savoy Hotel
8. Santa Isabel Hotel
9. Madeira Sheraton Hotel
10. Reid's Hotel
11. Main Hospital
12. Football Stadia
13. Quinta Magnolia
AVENIDA LUIS CAMÕES
R. DE FAVILA
AVENIDA DO INFANTE
AV. DO INFANTE
RUA DO DR. PITA
C. DA CASA BRANCA
E. MONUMENTAL
R Seco
R. IMPERATRIZ
D. AMELIA
R. CARVALHO ARAUJO
Santa
Catarina
Gardens
AVENIDA SA CARNEIRO
ESTRADA DA PONTINHA
CAIS NOVO
MOLHE
DA PONTINHA
N

Adjoining the Quinta das Cruzes is the **Conve**
(Saint Clare's Convent) founded at the end of th
The inside of this delightful church is decora
(glazed tiles) similar to a mosque. The lofty ce
adorned, too — nothing is sombre here. Look
supported by lions and surmounted by a canop
shady cloisters are the tombstones of Zarco's two grand-daughters who founded the original convent. It was from this convent that the nuns fled from invading pirates to a mountain valley (see page 126). The convent is now a school and you are likely to see happy children playing midst the orange trees in the worn courtyard.

The next place of interest is westwards, up Rua da Carreira, to a street on the right called Rua do Quebra Costas, where hidden behind a wall is the **English Church,** built in 1822 as a Consular Church. According to Portuguese law at that time, the building must not look like a church, so although it has a dome this church has no spire or bell tower. The inside of the church, designed by Henry Veitch, who was the Consul General, has a look of the Temple over the Holy Sepulchre in Jerusalem: the central dome has an all-seeing eye which looks down on the congregation. A restful garden surrounds the church, where stands a bronze bust of Philippa of Lancaster, Princess of England and Queen of Portugal. She was the mother of Prince Henry the Navigator. The present chaplain, Canon Walter, and Mrs Walter are always glad to receive visitors and pre-lunch refreshments are served in the garden on Sundays, after the 1100 hrs service (see page 51).

Above and westwards is an old fortress, **Fortaleza do Pico,** the peak fortress, which is now used as a radio station: at night this ancient building is floodlit and can be seen at its best from the Madeira Casino Nightclub.

Back on the Rua da Carreira we can walk down the Rua dos Aranhas, back to Avenida Arriaga and the centre of the city.

The western outskirts of Funchal

At the western end of Avenida Arriaga is **Praça do Infante,** the busy roundabout with a central fountain. The wide main road going west up the hill is Avenida do Infante, one of the few modern roads in Madeira, with fast moving traffic. You may like to pause a while in the **Santa Catarina gardens;** they make the steep hill less of a climb, and from here you have a good view over the harbour. Take

., by the small lake and watch the swans, there is a children's .ayground, too. The little chapel, Santa Catarina, dates from Zarco's times and is one of the oldest buildings on the island: it is now a small museum. Nearby is a statue of Christopher Columbus.

Across the road the building that looks so attractive is the **Hospicio Maria Amelia.** It was a gift from the Dowager Empress of Brazil, whose daughter, Princess Maria, died of consumption in 1853. The building was opened in 1862 as a hospital for the poor who suffered with consumption. It was built with two wings, one for men and one for women, and in between there is a chapel. There is a sad story that Maximilian, who later became Emperor of Mexico, fell in love with this doomed Brazilian princess and visited her in Madeira; it is a fact that he gave a sculpture of Our Lady of Sorrows, with a gold heart round her neck, to the hospice. The Dowager Empress made her sister, Queen Mary of Sweden, a trustee of this hospice, and recently in 1986 the present King and Queen of Sweden visited the hospice when in Madeira.

Continuing up the hill, on your right are various shops and a supermarket, while on the sea side you pass **Quinta Vigia,** a notable old building painted pink and white. It is the official residence of the President of the Regional Government. Now you are reaching the beginning of the big hotel area. First there is the modern **Casino Park Hotel** and seawards is the **Madeira Casino,** which houses a cinema, restaurant, coffee bar, gambling room and, at the top, a night club with a most splendid view over the city, especially at night. In a cluster you will locate the **Savoy Hotel** with the **Santa Isabel Hotel** next door, and round the corner, past a garage, the **Madeira Sheraton,** a very comfortable and friendly place to stay. Here, too, are several restaurants.

The story of the Madeira Sheraton is worth telling: it is the story of Manuel de Sousa Pestana, a man who realised his dream. At the beginning, Manuel and Caridade were young friends in a poor farming community. As they grew up Manuel fell in love with the sweet Caridade but because of his position in life he did not declare his love; instead he worked seven days a week on the land, saved his earnings and then opened a market stall in the village. So hard did he work that he soon had sufficient money to buy a ticket to South Africa. There he worked on a communal farm and saved to buy a small grocery shop. Eventually he prospered sufficiently for him to return to claim his bride and take her back to South Africa. A son was born and each year they returned to Madeira to see their families. So great was his success and determination that he was eventually able to return to live in Madeira. He then decided to build a five-star hotel and he invited Sheraton to lend its name. Today the Madeira Sheraton is the only privately-owned hotel in the Sheraton group. Because he had created thousands of jobs on the island, Portugal decided to honour this hard-working and conscientious man. On 20 November 1972 the Portuguese Government bestowed on Manuel de Sousa Pestana their highest award for achievement, the title of Commendor. The Pestana family still take a lively interest in the running of their excellent hotel.

Should you be driving a car around this area, it is worth noting that the Avenida do Infante has two lane traffic and it is forbidden to turn across the flow of traffic. You must continue until you can use a junction.

Madeira's main **hospital** is along the Avenida Luis Camoes, and is reached from Avenida do Infante via Ruia do Favila. The next main road you come to after Avenida do Infante, which turns inland, is the Rua do Dr Pita, and it is along here that you find the big football stadium and the **Quinta Magnolia.** This charming country estate was once the British Country Club but is now a hotel school. The main house has been reconstructed to make a distinctive dining room and bar with verandah. You may have lunch here from Monday to Saturday. The bar opens at 1200 and lunch is at 1300 hrs, teatime is 1600 hrs. You need to telephone 64614 in advance as tables for lunch have to be reserved, but not for tea. Advanced students serve at table, supervised by monitors. There is a daily menu of specially prepared dishes with a choice for each course. Outside are lovely gardens, swimming pool and tennis courts that are open to the public.

The Botanical Gardens

There are several ways of reaching the **Jardim Botanico,** the Botanical Gardens. If you engage a taxi, he will use short cuts up very steep inclines to climb the high hills at the back of the city. The single taxi fare from the city is 700 escudos (£3). If you are on a coach excursion the driver will have to take a different route, avoiding the narrow streets. To go by public bus you should take a number 30, marked Jardim Botanico: it goes once an hour from the bus station along the Avenida do Mar. If you are driving yourself follow the east bank of the Ribeira de João Gomes, the Rua Dr Manuel Pestana Junior; it goes north out of the city and is signposted to Camacha. This very winding road turns into the Estrada V Cacongo, then the Caminho do Meio. The Botanical Gardens are signposted and are on the left hand side of the Caminho das Voltas. The gardens are open from Monday to Saturday, 0800 to 1800 hrs (but it is advisable to check these times with the Tourist Office as they may vary). Entrance costs 200 escudos (£0.87), children under 14 half price.

You may be surprised to know that it was only in 1950 that it was decided to start Botanical Gardens in Madeira. For many years before that the owners of the great *quintas* had used their country estate grounds to plant exotic trees and plants, obtained from all over the world. So by using the Quinta do Bom Sucesso, where the Reid family had built a lovely house surrounded by large gardens and farmland, the Botanical Gardens had an ideal place to commence.

The gardens are situated 200 to 350 metres above sea level, and differing temperatures are created behind the *quinta* walls. Since they were first opened, the grounds have been extended to an area of 150,000 square metres, of which 25,000 are gardens and park. The gardens are preserving over 150 endemic plants and a study is being made of the native flora of the island. The plants, trees and flowers are all labelled in Portuguese and Latin. Little gravel paths lead to most parts of the garden, but some slopes can be slippery in moist weather.

One of the most pleasant things about this colourful place is the situation overlooking Funchal. The design of the grounds affords extensive views over the city below. The air is fragrant with the perfume of the beds of roses and other sweet flowers. Little pools of waterlilies and fish blend with banks of exotic desert cactus; orchids and rain forest plants thrive inside steaming greenhouses. Pleasant, too is a little tea garden for light refreshments and there are toilets. The *quinta* is now a meteorological observatory and museum.

The Botanical Gardens are certainly worth a visit, even if you are not a keen botanist, for it is a peaceful place where no one hurries, and only the birds in the trees create a noise. Disappointingly, there is no brochure in English describing the floral delights to be seen.

Your tour of Funchal is now over. You could finish in style with a visit to **Reid's Hotel,** maybe for afternoon tea. Reid's was one of the first hotels to offer British and world wide visitors the very best service. Not everyone wants or is able to stay in such luxury, but it does underline the way that the Madeiran people are prepared to make themselves hospitable. The smaller hotels and pensions located in and around Funchal also show this to be true.

Exploring Funchal and its environs can be hard on the feet and mind, but several of the places described in these chapters can be reached by taxi. Do try and see as much as your time allows, for Funchal, while being thoroughly Portuguese, has a character and atmosphere that is unique. Always close in the background of this great city are the high, green mountains, with their fresh Atlantic air and, we hope, lots of sunshine for you.

The world-famous Reid's Hotel is the ideal place for a cup of tea in luxurious surroundings after a tour of Funchal.
(Photo J.A. Deneulain)

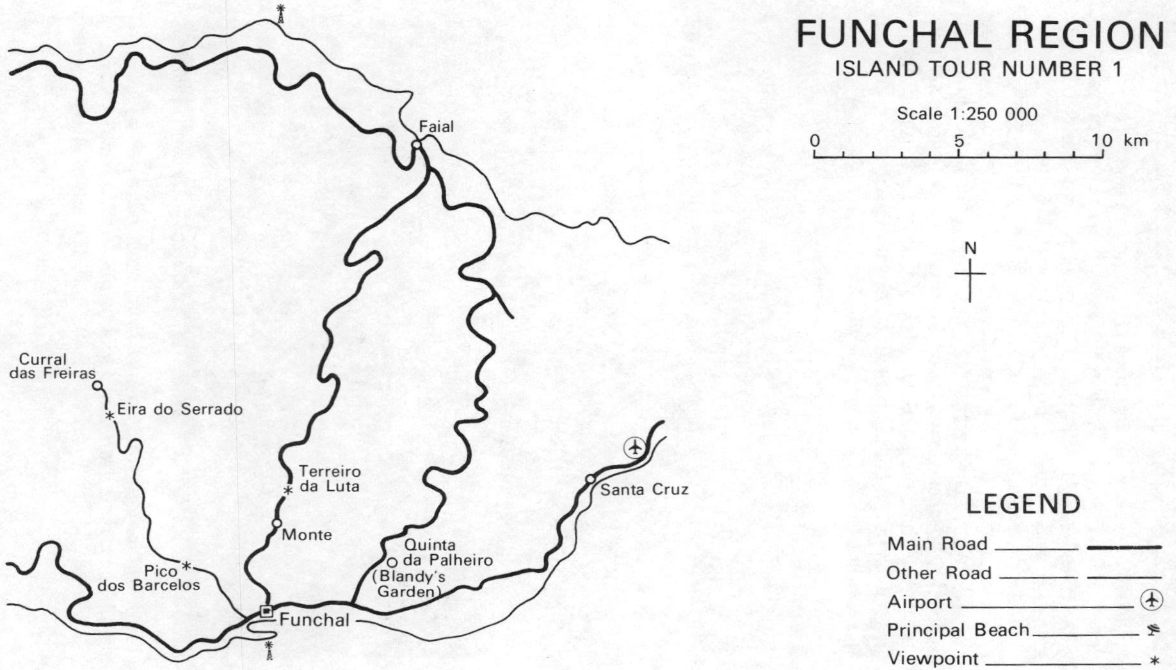

FUNCHAL REGION

ISLAND TOUR NUMBER 1

Scale 1:250 000

0 5 10 km

N

Faial
Curral das Freiras
Eira do Serrado
Terreiro da Luta
Monte
Pico dos Barcelos
Quinta da Palheiro (Blandy's Garden)
Funchal
Santa Cruz

LEGEND

Main Road
Other Road
Airport
Principal Beach
Viewpoint *

TEN

The Funchal region

Madeira is not a particularly large island, but when it comes to touring the countryside by road there is plenty to see and interest the visitor. The island's terrain is mostly mountainous with deep ravines in between, and many of the roads wind tortuously up one side of a valley and then down again on the other side, which can make driving very slow. Added to this, some of the roads are narrow with sharp bends and, especially in the north and west, the poor surfaces make travel very tiring. However, do not be deterred; after all most people come to Madeira mainly to explore this beautiful verdant island with its many high peaks, deep green forests, pleasant fertile valleys and pretty villages.

Touring the island

If you want to see all over the island you will need several days, even a week would not be too long. But for the benefit of those holidaymakers who can spare only a short time, this guide suggests three full-day tours plus a half-day trip, to complement the sightseeing in Funchal described in the previous chapter. In the case of the whole day tours, you will need to leave your hotel about 0830 hrs and will not get back before 1830 hrs. This schedule allows stops of about fifteen minutes at viewpoints, perhaps thirty minutes for refreshment breaks, plus an hour and a half for lunch. All the tours commence in Funchal. Sometimes it is necessary to cover part of the same route twice to reach the final destination, but this has been avoided as much as possible.

The Tourist Office has maps and booklets that give suggested routes. Remember that darkness falls quickly in Madeira and your speed of travel will only average 20 mph. Bear in mind, too, the fact that petrol stations are far apart.

Island tour 1

Funchal — Pico dos Barcelos — Eira do Serrado — Curral das Freiras — Monte — Funchal. About 60km; half day.

This is a popular drive that can be enjoyed either in the morning or the afternoon, and it can be done in reverse order.

Leaving Funchal, take the road ER215, signed to São Martinho. This road is narrow until it leaves the city. You will see the hospital and the cemetery on your left. (Hopefully a bypass road of Funchal will soon be completed, so speeding up the flow of through traffic.)

Passing banana plantations, papaya groves and vineyards, the road starts to climb until it reaches the **Pico dos Barcelos** (335m) a notable viewpoint that is used by both coach and taxi excursions. Here you have extensive vistas all round Funchal to the east and Câmara de Lobos to the west; down below are the waving leaves of the bananas and the bell tower of São Martinho, a comparatively newly-built church. As well as this pictorial vista there are a number of souvenir stalls, and a restaurant with beds of colourful flowers. Pico dos Barcelos is one of the scenes of firework displays at Christmas time.

This route, now via the ER107, has to climb another six hundred metres into the mountains, through forests and along cobbled roads, in a series of spectacular hairpin bends. It is hard to realise that Funchal is only fourteen kilometres away.

When you reach **Eira do Serrado** it is another amazing look out point. All round you are the high peaks and mountain ridges, like Pico Grande (1657m) and Pico Ruivo (1861m), while down below in the valley is the tiny village of **Curral das Freiras** (the Nuns' Shelter). A story tells of the days long past when, in 1566, pirates raided the Convent of Saint Clare in Funchal. To avoid a fate worse than death the nuns fled along the coast and up the ravine into the high mountains to hide away, for Curral das Freiras is the only village that cannot be seen from the sea. Later a settlement grew there, for the rich volcanic soil proved to be fertile. From the mirador above you can look down on this tiny village and wonder at the hazards the brave nuns had to encounter to reach this haven of safety.

Before you descend to this village you may care to have a drink at the little bar inside the souvenir shop. Why not try one of the

The richly decorated Igreja de Nossa Senhora do Monte with its many steps.

local drinks — perhaps *gingho,* which is made from the cherries that grow in the Curral Valley? Another speciality are the sweets flavoured with eucalyptus leaves and fennel. You can buy souvenirs here. There are thick woollen jumpers and cardigans that cost from 2000 escudos (£8.69); colourful tiles made into cheese boards for about 900 escudos (£3.90); and bright red clay cockerels in various sizes, which make a cheerful present. These are the national emblem of Portugal. You can descend on foot down a winding road to the village, which is in an extinct volcanic crater. There you will see the little church the nuns built to Saint Francis, in thankfulness for their safe deliverance. The road to the village is about a kilometre in length, and it was not completed until 1959. There is also a recommended walk from Picos dos Barcelos to Curral das Freiras.

You have to return along the same route, the ER107. Note the sturdy chestnut trees in this area; there is a special chestnut festival here in the autumn. Look for a road junction on the left signed for Monte the ER105. You can avoid a return to Funchal by taking this inland route — from Funchal you would need the ER103 to get to Monte.

Just six kilometres north of Funchal, **Monte** (550m) was once a garrison town for the British Army. In the nineteenth and twentieth centuries wealthy visitors from Europe built fine *quintas* (estates) and the area became very fashionable on account of its fine clean air and splendid views of the city below. In 1921 the exiled Emperor of Austria, Charles I, lived here in the Quinta de Monte with his wife and seven children. Unfortunately he died two years later and was buried in the church, **Igreja de Nossa Senhora do Monte** (Our Lady of the Mountains).

During the Second World War, there were of course no visitors and the Victorian funicular railway connecting Funchal with Monte was discontinued. Today on one side of the tree-lined square, Largo do Fonte, you can see the former station and railway bridge. Below are beautiful gardens, laid out in 1894 and still kept in the style of gardens of that era, with small clipped box hedges and neat little stone covered pathways. Also in this large square is a café with toilets and a few souvenirs.

To reach the church you must take a short walk uphill along a cobblestone path, which overlooks the gardens. Well established tall trees make this a shady place. The imposing church, set high on a mount, has a flight of seventy-four steps and on Assumption Day, 15 August, many islanders make a pilgrimage to their patron saint. Some climb these steps on their knees. The church was built in the eighteenth century on the site of a chapel first erected in 1470 by Adam Goncalves Ferreira and his sister Eve, the first twins to be born in Madeira. The present church has twin-domed bell towers, a Baroque pediment and many windows by the side of the arcaded porch. This makes a striking facade against the blue sky. Inside, the tomb of the Emperor Charles of Austria is on the left hand side. Above the altar in a silver tabernacle is the tiny cloaked figure of Our Lady of the Mount.

(Opposite) *The flower sellers in Madeira are always dressed in folk costume and look as colourful as the flowers they sell.*

At the foot of the church stairway you see the departure point for the **toboggan run** from Monte to Funchal. The *carros de cesto* are wickerwork seats on wood and metal runners; once they were used by the Madeirans to slide their farm produce down the steep cobbled slopes of the mountain to Funchal market; sometimes they were drawn by bullocks. Nowadays the *carros* are a prime tourist attraction and many holidaymakers feel their visit to Madeira would not be complete without this thrilling experience. Each *carro* holds two people and at a cost of 1400 escudos (£6) you can sit in one of the upholstered seats while two men dressed in white with straw hats and rubber soled boots guide the *carros* by means of two ropes down the steep, slippery, cobbled streets at an ever increasing speed, using only their feet and strength to get you round the bends.

It is quite a perilous ride and not for the faint-hearted, but no one who has experienced the ride ever admits to being scared, and for the most it is a memorable adventure. At the bottom of the run the toboggan men hope for a tip, then with the toboggans, they all pile into a truck to be taken up the hill again to wait for their next dash down with a load of squealing tourists. You will be surprised to see that some very venerable men will be working the *carros de cesto*.

Should you wish for a souvenir of this exciting event, you could buy yourself a replica of the toboggan men's straw hat. They are sold in many souvenir shops at a cost of about 500 escudos (£2.17) and they make good sunhats. You can also commence a similar toboggan ride from higher up the mountain at Terreiro da Luta (see Tour Three), which runs along the course of the old railway track, Caminho do Comboio as far as Monte and costs 900 escudos (£3.91) each.

If you do not wish to walk back up the hill to Monte and where you left your car you should be able to get a taxi.

We rather fancy that you will enjoy the sophistication of modern travel as you drive down to **Funchal.**

(Opposite) Top: *Carro de cesto, the toboggan ride, is one of Madeira's major tourist attractions.*
Bottom: *Palm trees line the road down to the old quay, Porto Santo.*

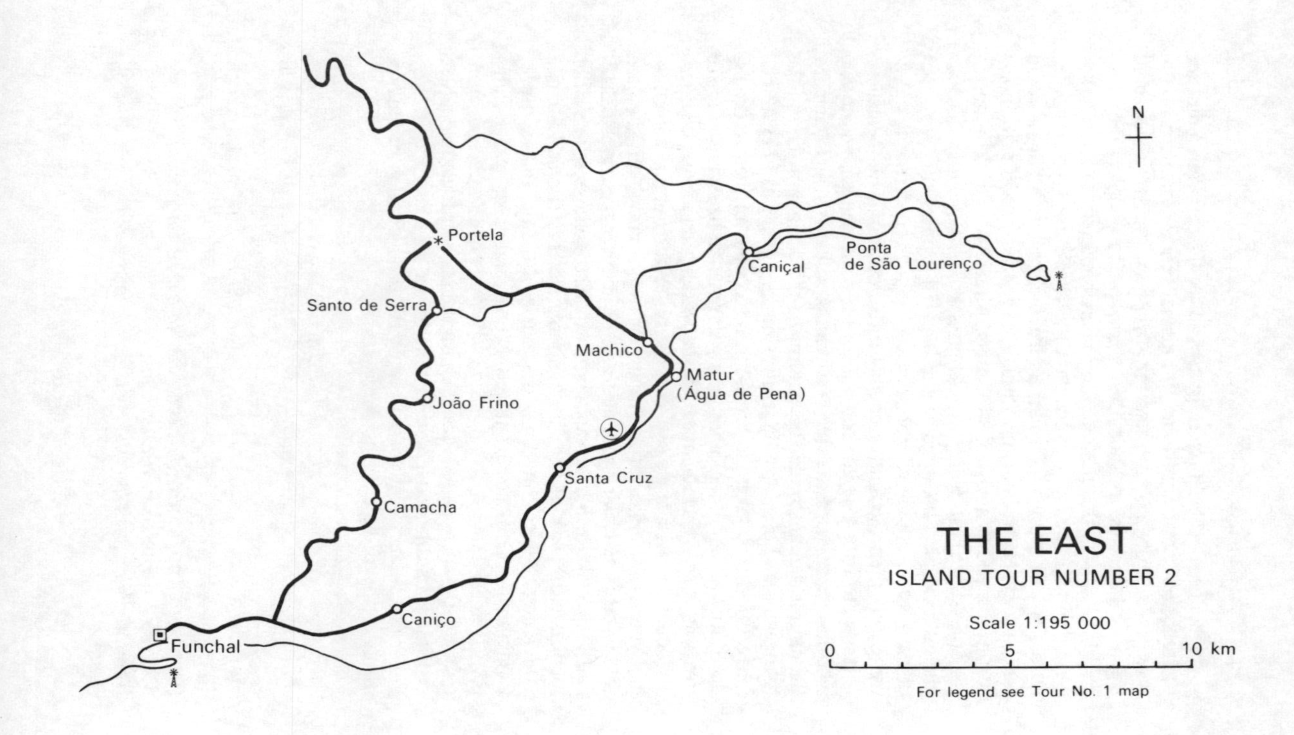
N
Portela
Santo de Serra
Caniçal
Ponta
de São Lourenço
Machico
Matur
(Água de Pena)
João Frino
Santa Cruz
Camacha
Caniço
Funchal
THE EAST
ISLAND TOUR NUMBER 2
Scale 1:195 000
0
5
10 km
For legend see Tour No. 1 map

ELEVEN

The east

Island tour 2

Funchal — Caniço — Santa Cruz — Matur — Machico — Caniçal — Ponta de São Lourenço — Machico — Santo da Serra — Portela — João Frino — Camacha — Blandy's Gardens — Funchal. About 95 Kilometres; full day.

Leave Funchal driving eastwards on the ER105. Traffic will be heavy until you reach the outskirts of the city. On the way you pass many fine old houses *(quintas)* and, although many are hidden by tall walls, you may be able to glimpse well established gardens full of sub-tropical flowers such as the colourful bougainvillea, poinsettias, oleanders and huge canna lilies. Hanging plants and window boxes add yet more colour, while wrought iron balconies and sheltered patios, ferns and garden statues recall a graceful bygone age.

Out of town the road winds close by the sea along a high cliff. Looking backwards you will have a good view of Funchal and the harbour in the bay below. Watch out for the local buses that expect to have the right of way and sometimes travel very fast. By the time you reach the turning for **Garajau** (by a petrol station) you are in quieter countryside and can start to enjoy the sea views.

You may continue on the ER101 or turn south downhill to Garajau, when you will pass the Inter Atlas Hotel and some modern villas and houses. Set on a headland is a large statue of Christ with outstretched arms, similar to the one to be seen near Lisbon. Here it is a very steep drop down of a thousand metres to visit the small stony beach of **Ponta do Garajau.** The pleasant road then twists and turns its way past banana plantations for a further two kilometres, until you drive down a narrow one-way street to find yourself in the main square of **Caniço,** a village noted for its onions. Visible from afar is the distinctive eighteenth-century church with its tall pointed spire and clock tower. There are several *typico* restaurants in or near this village and plenty of taxis to get you there and back, if at any time you do not wish to drive.

Return now to the ER101 road, signposted to the airport, which bypasses **Santa Cruz.** Should you wish to stop in this town you must turn right towards the church and town hall. It is an important district centre with a market.

Soon you have a quick sight of the end of the airport runway which is so near to the sea. In fact the road you are on goes beneath the runway and you drive through the support pillars for the concrete many metres above the road. Next you come to the **Matur** holiday complex, and you cannot fail to see the huge white modern block of the five-star Atlantis Hotel, a real eyesore of a building. This is a popular holiday resort for the 'young in heart', who prefer to have an active and entertaining time, rather than a more sedate and quiet vacation at somewhere like Reid's or the Savoy.

Twenty-six kilometres from Funchal is **Machico.** You have the best view of the town when you approach it this way from the west. Set in a wide bay with cliffs either side, the town nestles in the centre. Anyone with a liking for a legend will remember that it is here that the ill-fated lovers Robert Machim and Anne d'Arset were supposed to have been shipwrecked (see chapter eight), and where João Gonçalves Zarco and Tristão Vaz Teixeira actually landed in 1419. The large four-star Dom Pedro Hotel is built at this western end of the bay, a short downhill drive to the town centre.

Machico is an important fishing port. Once it was the first government headquarters of the Madeira archipelago and a boat building centre. Even today you are likely to see a vessel on the stocks in the yard. At the mouth of a fertile valley, Machico is divided by a river, the Ribeira Machico that flows out to sea. The fishermen's old quarters, the **Banda d'Alem,** lie on the east side with the old town to the west. The imposing Manueline parish church, built at the end of the fifteenth century, stands in the central square. In front of the church is a statue of Tristão Vaz Teixeira, who ruled this eastern region so long ago. Today in the plaza tall plane trees give shade and passers-by gaze at the lovely rose window and ornate carved doorway of the church, the **Igreja Matriz de Machico.**

If you have difficulty in parking near the centre of the town then turn down one of the tiny side streets (some are one way only) towards the seafront and the large pebble beach. Gaily painted boats lie in-shore and there is a fine view eastwards to the headland. It is delightful to wander the narrow cobbled streets leading back

Tristao Vas Teixeira stands proudly in the centre of Machico, the town he founded.

from the seafront, which contain an assortment of small shops appealing to tourists and locals alike. Look for number 13; in the window is a collection of old wine bottles covered in cobwebs! Restaurants and cafés have tables and chairs outside and it is a nice place for a chat, refreshments or lunch.

As you walk over the river bridge take a look at the lovely gardens on the east side; they are a riot of colour. On the east bank is a small dark looking chapel, the **Senhor dos Milagres.** Around 1420 a small chapel was constructed on the site of the tomb of the legendary English lovers. It was rebuilt in the sixteenth century and in 1803 was badly damaged by floods when the image of the Senhor dos Milagres was washed out to sea. A seaman on an American ship saw the image floating and it was eventually recovered and returned to the Chapel. There is a story that in 1825 Robert Page, an English merchant, claimed that he had found in this Chapel the cedar wood cross that originally stood upon the grave of Robert Machim and Anne d'Arset.

There are two forts in Machico, the Fort of São João Baptista is near the port and the other one, the Fort of Nossa Senhora do Amparo is on the seafront at the western end of the town. In the olden days bonfires were lit on the surrounding hills to warn of the approach of pirates. One peak is called Pico de Facho (peak of the torch).

Two important religious festivals take place in Machico. The festival of the Holy Sacrament is celebrated on the last Sunday in August with a procession. Festivities begin the day before when the surrounding hills are lit by colourful electric lamps and torches. Then on the nights of 8th and 9th October there is a procession for Senhor dos Milagres, when the statue of Senhor dos Milagres is carried to and from the chapel to the church, led by torches.

Leave Machico on the road to Caniçal. Once more the road climbs high into the hills, with good views of the valley, and eventually you drive through Madeira's longest tunnel (800m), completed in 1950. Watch out for oncoming traffic as the tunnel is not always lit. Reaching the eastern end of the tunnel you feel you have arrived in a different land, for here the landscape has changed from verdant green to a desolate ochre-coloured earth.

Caniçal is the most easterly village in Madeira. Once busy with the whaling industry, the factory now lies idle. It has only fishing and a little farming to support its people. Because of its outlying situation the way of life is simple and traditional. Do not be surprised when you see the hay being cut with hand-held sickles, a job for several entire families.

The beautiful church in Caniçal, the most easterly village in Madeira, is well worth a visit.

A narrow road winding above the village goes out to a headland known as **Ponta de São Lourenço,** a refreshing way out vista. Some coach excursions reach this point and disgorge their passengers, who then scramble over the dry grassy rocks to admire the extensive views out to sea. At the extreme tip off-shore are the small islands of Ilhéu de Agostinho and tiny Ilhéu de Fora, which has a lighthouse. Close by the end of the road is a track leading down to **Prainha** where you can see Madeira's only sandy beach. Do not get too excited! The sand is blackish and the shore small. Close to Ponto Rosto is a building which was erected recently for a French film company and now lies derelict.

Before you return to your car it is probable that you will admire a local artisan patiently carving whalebone ornaments. His pitch is by a small refeshment stall. These hand made replicas of the now protected whale make a delightful souvenir and it is good to support a local craftsman. Prices start around 2,000 escudos (£8.69).

Now it is necessary to retrace the route back as far as Machico, then take the inland road up by the river valley and its banana plantations, into the wooded hills towards Ribeira do Machico. This is a wonderful drive with the air full of eucalyptus, pines, laurel and other aromatic trees and shrubs. Ferns and flowers deck the hedge rows and if you stop to take a photograph, bird song will greet your ears.

After about five kilometres look left for a minor road leading to **Santo da Serra,** another three kilometres drive. Built on a forest plateau at an altitude of 800m, this is a country resort for the residents of Funchal. The wide market square is not particularly beautiful, but allows plenty of space for parking. Here you can have lunch at the old *pousada* (hotel) which is located near to the wrought iron gates that lead into the Quinta da Junta Park.

Formerly the property of the Blandy family, this lovely old estate is now government property and a national park. Try to spare time for a walk in the grounds, there is no charge. Have a look at the solid old house, then walk down the avenue of well laid out and landscaped gardens to a belvedere which gives a panoramic view of the Machico valley, and in clear weather even as far as Porto Santo. On the way back you will see a herd of deer, some wild ponies and ornamental birds including peacocks. There is a children's play park and football pitch, too.

Nothing much in the way of tourist shops here, but there are two butcher's shops which could be useful if you are self-catering. Santo da Serra is famous these days for its nine-hole golf course. You do

This imposing Quinta stands in the Park at Santo da Serra.

not need to be a member of the club to play. The clubhouse bar is in the old *pousada* building, and is now quite run down with an air of faded glory.

Having been well refreshed with food and walking and provided you have the time, continue on the road northwards for a further five kilometres to the **Portela Pass** (the gateway) 625m high. Here at the crossroads you will find a bar, a restaurant (good for *espetada),* toilets and a fine viewpoint. Souvenir stalls sell Portuguese woollen garments, hats, clothes and other small items for the tourists.

Returning by the ER102 and driving south towards Funchal, you'll find that the well made road allows for faster travel. It is still wooded with small areas under cultivation. From **João Frino** the road to Camacha is narrow and once more you find many bends and blind corners as you make your way up and down ravines, full of lush vegetation and small homesteads that cling to the sides of the hills.

Camacha, at an altitude of 700m, is at the heart of the willow industry which employs over two thousand workers who make the sturdy furniture, baskets, trays and other useful items for which Camacha is famous. Before you reach the village you will probably have seen fields of willows. These are not at all like the weeping willow trees in English gardens, but more like bushes for they are kept short. Each year after the young shoots have grown sturdy in early spring, they are cut right down to the base. These shoots are put in hot water to soften, then peeled and left outside for four or five months to dry. Some of the wicker is put into cold water before peeling so producing a different coloured cane, which is used as a contrast in the work. Genuine wicker work from Madeira is always worked by hand and none of the basket work ever has any nails or screws to secure it. Most of the work is done as a cottage industry. In the damper valleys in the north and around Camacha, it is a familiar sight to see bunches of cane stacked outside or on the roofs to dry or waiting to be used.

In the centre of Camacha a large factory is open to the public, where visitors can see some of the villagers at work. In a large sale room crammed with wicker items tourists can select their own handmade goods. It is said that over 1,200 models are made and much of the production (over 900 tonnes annually) is exported abroad especially to the USA and Europe. Prices at the factory are reasonable and holidaymakers are able to put their unwrapped purchases in the hold of the aircraft returning home.

Above the wicker work factory in Camacha is a large restaurant, where on Sundays groups of folk dancers and musicians perform.

Camacha is also famous for the flowers grown in the area, and all the flower girls in local costume who sit outside the Cathedral in Funchal come from the village of Camacha. Several of the *levada* walks, which are detailed so well in the book *Landscapes of Madeira* (see Bibliography) start at Camacha. In addition, walk number 7 in the Tourist Office Handbook shows the route from Camacha to Monte, along the Levada dos Tomos, a 12km walk that takes about four hours and is described as suitable for walkers of all ages.

Leaving Camacha on the ER102 signposted Funchal, you now drop down quite rapidly along a pretty road, sometimes described as Paradise Valley.

Should you be doing this tour in reverse order, you may like to make a small detour, which is signposted, to visit the delightful gardens at **Quinta Palheiro Ferreiro,** more commonly known as **Blandy's Gardens.** The gardens open in the morning only, Monday to Friday; you can purchase tickets at the gate. You park outside and then walk down the cobble drive to find yourself in part of a huge 800 acre private estate which once belonged to the Count of Carvahal and is now owned by the Blandy family, one of the foremost British families in Madeira.

This is one of the few places where there are sufficient level fields for cattle to graze. In other parts of Madeira the animals are kept and fed in sheds, only coming out occasionally for exercise.

Here at Palheiro Gardens you enter a bygone atmosphere of the great *quintas.* Gracious lawns lead from the Blandy house down landscaped terraces to clumps of rare trees and plants; birds, bees and butterflies live here too. Great masses of camellias, magnolias and well established bowers of roses, together with herbaceous plants and a little stream, makes this a rare treat for garden lovers. The 30-acre flower garden has many pleasures not the least of which is the fact that it is not too tidy, for here and there you come across nettles and weeds, which give it a homely lived-in atmosphere. Rather sadly the original *quinta* owned by the Count is now in a state of disrepair and it is hoped that in time it can be restored to its previous glory; it would make a splendid botanical museum.

It is just five kilometres from these gardens to the centre of **Funchal,** via the ER102 and ER101. You will probably curse the traffic hold ups as you reach the market area, but be patient and recall your day amidst the green mountains and hidden valleys of the eastern countryside.

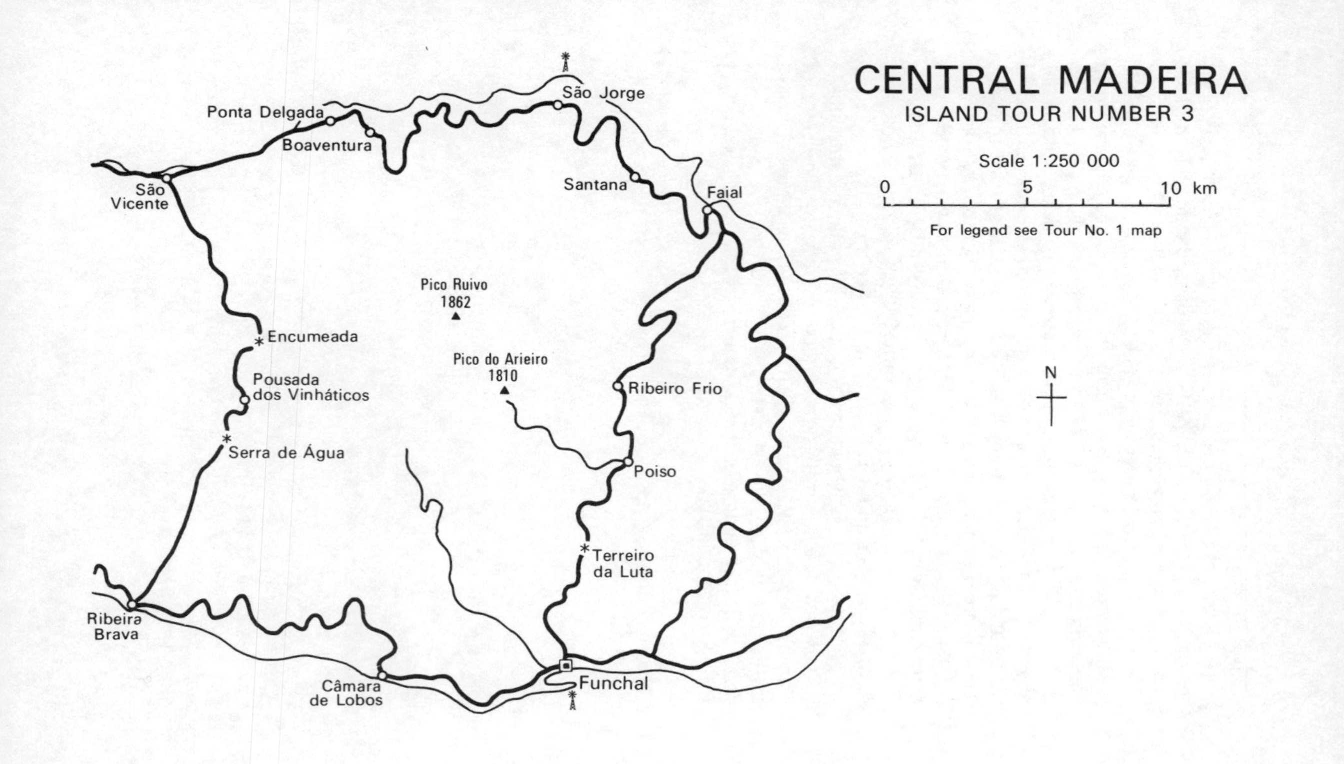
CENTRAL MADEIRA
ISLAND TOUR NUMBER 3
Scale 1:250 000
0
5
10 km
For legend see Tour No. 1 map
N
Ponta Delgada
São Jorge
Boaventura
Santana
Faial
São Vicente
Pico Ruivo 1862
Encumeada
Pico do Arieiro 1810
Pousada dos Vinháticos
Ribeiro Frio
Serra de Água
Poiso
Terreiro da Luta
Ribeira Brava
Câmara de Lobos
Funchal

TWELVE

Central Madeira

Island tour 3

Funchal — Terreiro da Luta — Poiso — Pico do Arieiro — Ribeiro Frio — Faial — Santana — São Jorge — Boaventura — Ponta Delgada — São Vicente — Encumeada — Pousada dos Vinhaticos — Serra de Água — Ribeira Brava — Câmara de Lobos — Funchal. About 147 kilometres; full day.

Leave **Funchal** by the ER103, signposted to Monte and Terreiro da Luta. You will climb surprisingly quickly out of the city. Do not stop at Monte (see Tour One) but continue to **Terreiro da Luta** where it is worth a brief stop, because here at the café terrace in clear weather you can have an excellent view of Funchal. You can also look at Madeira's largest monument which stands here on a plinth, near a small chapel. It is dedicated to Our Lady of Peace, Nossa Senhora da Paz, and was completed in 1927. It is said to be built on the spot where our Lady of the Mount once appeared to the people of Madeira. Round the base of the statue are heavy anchor chains weighed by large stones. The chains are from ships that were torpedoed and sunk by the Germans in Funchal harbour during the war; one wonders at the great effort required to get these heavy objects up the steep slopes. It is here that the old funicular railway ran from Funchal. Now you can take a toboggan ride down.

Proceeding northwards, still on the ER103, the road soon climbs up to the **Poiso** pass and a junction of three roads. If you have started your drive early in the morning and the weather is clear, then this is the day to make an important detour, by turning left on to the ER202 towards **Pico do Arieiro.** This road follows the mountains and owing to the height the terrain is bare of trees: only sheep and goats graze the moorland. Beware, they often wander onto the road. You are now beginning to drive higher than some of the peaks and you will want to pause to take a photograph of the impressive deep tree-covered ravines below you. It is a wonderful experience to drive to the summit of this 1,818m-high mountain; it is hoped that the weather keeps clear so that you can enjoy its immense views and spectacular panorama.

Madeira, being of volcanic origin, has a fascinating landscape and its eruptions are clearly seen here at Pico do Arieiro. Time and weather have softened the rugged high peaks, nevertheless it is an awesome sight. Standing here, it is hard to realise that the city of Funchal is just 23kms below. In the clear, crisp air one has a god-like feeling, except that now and then a coach load of holidaymakers arrive, to scramble about and disturb the silence.

The mountain top is slowly becoming a major tourist attraction, now that a modern road to it has been constructed, and already a large *pousada* has been built and is about to open. The small café is always busy selling *bolo de mel,* the delicious long-lasting Madeiran molasses cake. Packed for export it has a similarity to Christmas cake and is guaranteed to keep for a year. Another speciality that is particularly good at Pico do Arieiro is a glass of *poncho,* Madeira's fiery drink, made with honey, lemon and brandy. It is especially warming should it be a cold day. If you are here to walk the mountains you will see the start of the walk from the view point. The pathway was constructed in 1960 and is much used by enthusiasts.

Returning to the car you now have to go back to Poiso, then continue northwards to **Ribeiro Frio** (Ribo Frio), the cold river, at an altitude of 800m, and its thick woods. Here too is a small carpark and toilets. A government owned trout hatchery is set in some lovely gardens, and there are tables and seats for picnics. This is the starting point for *levada* walks. Should you wish to have a quick look at the *levada* you can cross and walk back up the road from the carpark a few yards and enter a picnic area. At the far end you will see a fast flow of water down steep steps — a *levada.*

If it is time for refreshment a ten minute drive towards **Achada do Cedro Gordo** will bring you to more picnic tables and a restaurant.

Now you are getting towards the north and the road descends in a series of hairpin bends. This is a humid part of the island and you will see dense woods of laurels and pines; in the hedgerows, growing wild, the white *zantedeschia aethiopica* with its large green leaves looks similar to an arum lily. Nasturtiums meander and the blue or white *agapanthus africanus* stand tall. Willows, too, grow here. This is some of the most attractive of Madeira's countryside. Before

Terreiro da Luta. Funchal's largest monument, dedicated to our Lady of Peace *(see p.141).*

People still live in these attractive thatched cottages around Santana.

reaching Faial you will see a large restaurant called Casa de Chá (the Tea House), lying back off the road and with plenty of parking space. It is recommended for the regional cooking and good service.

At **Faial** we are on the north coast and the EN101. An attractive white church dominates this scene set amongst the sugar cane and vineyards. Here you have good views of the mighty Penha D'Aguia, the Eagle's Rock, which as one would expect from its name stands an impressive 590m high, with little white houses dotted in the valley below. You cross over the river bridge and climb up and round the Eagle's Rock; it is quite a hard drive but the views of the sea and village below are quite lovely. There is a view point (mirador) where you can stop to take a photograph — that is if it is not full up with cars!

Now you are approaching **Santana** and it is here that you begin to see the colourful little thatched cottages that are typical of the area. Whereas in other parts of the island these structures are used to house cattle, here many of the villagers make their home in the steeply pointed A-shaped structures. The Tourist Authority now hold competitions for the prettiest home and garden for this type of dwelling. Even the toilets at the local restaurant have been designed in the same shape. There is ample parking in Santana and it makes a pleasant place to stop for a meal. The O Colmo Restaurant has an interesting menu of local dishes, the service is fast and the dining room is pleasantly decorated.

Although at an altitude of 436m, the hills are full of apple trees and sugar cane; look out for the sweet potato plants — this vegetable will probably be served with your meal, too.

There is a five kilometre excursion that can be made from Santana to the **Parque das Queimadas,** a government forest park. From there it is possible to walk to the Casa das Queimadas, a rest house, where you can walk alongside a *levada* and it is also possible to picnic. Remember to take your cardigan as it can be cool. Be sure to wear suitable footwear as the paths may be slippery with moss.

Although Santana is only thirty-nine kilometres from Funchal and the distance can be driven in about two hours, it will most likely take you all morning to get there. So now you must decide whether to continue this long tour; the shorter alternative is to return to Faial and go back along the ER101, via Porto da Cruz and down to Portela, returning to Funchal by the Camacha road as described in Tour One.

Assuming that all is well and you do not mind the heights and bends and that you are enjoying the drive, from Santana you proceed westwards amongst the luscious green scenery. In spring time the yellow gorse and mimosa trees vie in glory; sturdy vines manage to grow when protected from the north winds by little fences. At **São Jorge** you see a church that was built in 1761.

From São Jorge to **Boaventura** the drive is a real adventure, for the road twists and winds its way along the north coast, then turns inland in a deep curve by Arco São Jorge (the arc). The Boaventura valley is more gentle, although the Atlantic rollers look quite wild and the place feels remote. There is a nice story about a Miss Turner who went to live at Santo da Serra, and there opened a Tea Room. Her gardener was always talking about his home village and asking her to visit, but she never did. However, before she died she left instructions that she wished to be buried there. Although it was a rough track, her coffin was carried over the mountains and she was buried in her gardener's village of Boaventura. In the cemetery a tombstone bears the name of a Miss Turner.

The next place you reach is the promontory of **Ponta Delgada.** Here it is possible to have a swim in a sea water swimming pool by the shore. Now the road is narrow, even cobbled, and goes below a high cliff. This can be very slow and is not for nervous drivers as meeting tour coaches can mean that you have to back up for some distance.

São Vicente is a pleasant sprawling coastal town. The river São Vicente flows out to sea here; a few shops and a restaurant make it a stopping place. The neat church is worth a visit for the interior is cool and decorated with scroll work and colourful Moorish tiles. It is restful after the hard driving. On this tour, from São Vicente, you leave the coast and turn southwards on the ER104, signposted Rosario and Ribeira Brava. There is a fine view of São Vicente as you climb away from the town, the red tiles and while walls of the clustered houses make an attractive picture. A chapel completed in 1953, the Church of Nossa Senhora de Fatima, has a fourteen metre high clocktower. Our Lady of Fatima is the patron saint of all Portugal.

Below in the valley and along the terraces every centimetre of ground is covered with crops. How green is the vista, broken only by great splashes of colour from the flower-bedecked cottages. Buzzards, kestrels, finches and canary birds fly overhead; all this is a naturalist's paradise. At the **Encumeada** summit (1,004m) there is a viewpoint where you can enjoy good vistas of both the north and south of Madeira.

Now the road descends into deep woods of laurel, bay and pines, so the air is fragrant and the scenery is magnificent with glimpses of deep ravines and clouds scurrying over the mountain tops.

Another popular stopping point is the attractive **Pousada dos Vinhaticos:** yet again you can climb a nearby hillock to a viewpoint for more photography. (Those who wish can walk from Encumeada to the Pousada, a distance of four kilometres, which takes about an hour and three quarters, and it is possible to stop for a picnic on the way.)

Your winding route drops quite fast down to Ribeira Brava, passing **Serra de Água,** with more terraces and red roofed cottages. Yellow oxalis fills the sides of the road as the valley reaches the sea at **Ribeira Brava.** This is an important stopping place for many of the coach excursions, and so the seafront has a line of stallholders selling souvenirs. On either side of the large village the mighty hills protect the houses from the wind; beside the main street the river flows steadily out to sea. As always in Madeiran towns and villages, the church is the focal point. Here standing in a black and white cobbled courtyard, is the sixteenth century church dedicated to Saint Benedict. The roof, flanked by a belfry, is decorated with blue and white tiles.

It is now only thirty kilometres to **Funchal** but you must allow at least an hour and a half to make this journey — hard to believe perhaps, but it is due to the narrow twisting road. You will on your way there pass interesting places such as **Câmara de Lobos,** but these are described at the beginning of the day drive in Tour Four and by now your mind and body will be too full of all you have enjoyed on this wonderful central tour to take in any more.

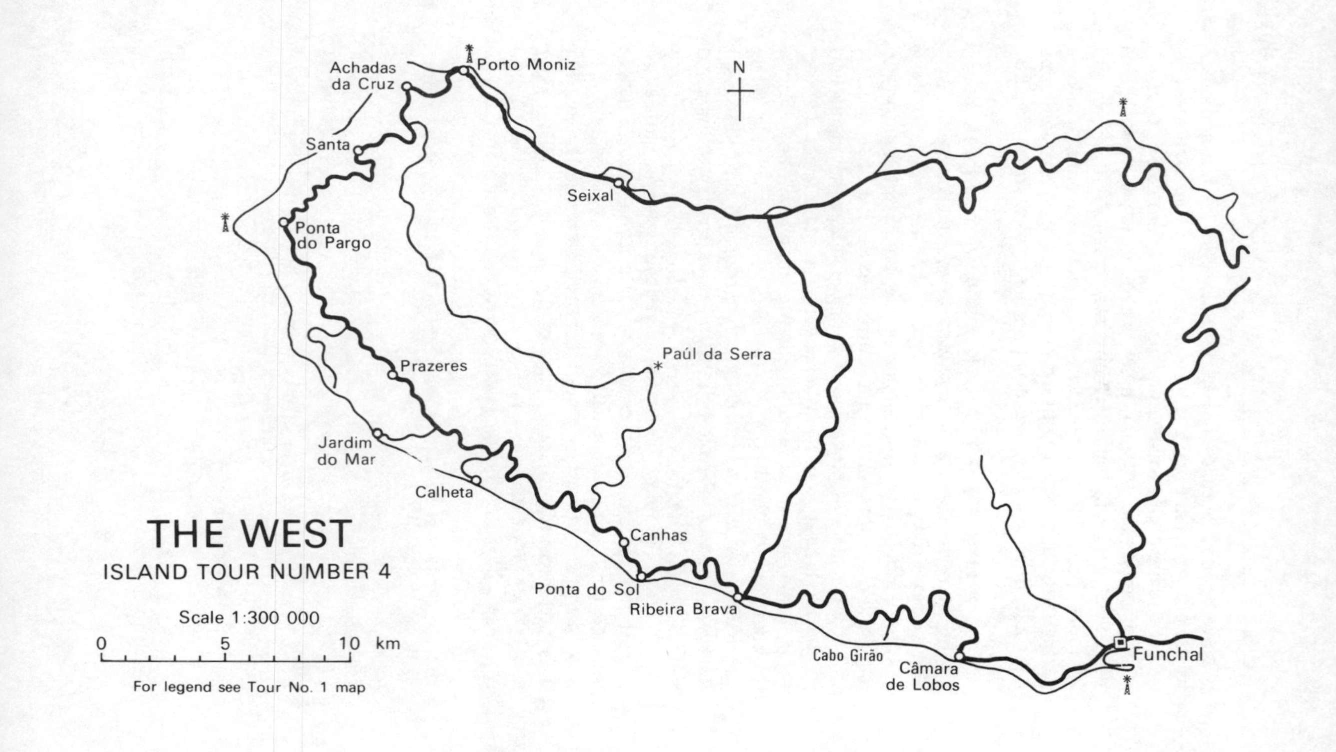
THE WEST
ISLAND TOUR NUMBER 4
Scale 1:300 000
0
5
10 km
For legend see Tour No. 1 map
N
Porto Moniz
Achadas
da Cruz
Santa
Ponta
do Pargo
Seixal
Paúl da Serra
Prazeres
Jardim
do Mar
Calheta
Canhas
Ponta do Sol
Ribeira Brava
Cabo Girão
Câmara
de Lobos
Funchal

THIRTEEN

The west

Island tour 4

Funchal — Camara de Lobos — Cabo Girão — Ribeira Brava — Ponta do Sol — Canhas — Paúl da Serra — Porto Moniz — Seixal — Achadas da Cruz — Ponto do Pargo — Prazeres — Estreito da Calheta — Canhas — Ribeira Brava — Funchal. About 210 kilometres; full day.

From Funchal you drive westwards on the ER101, signposted Câmara de Lobos. For a short way you will pass by banana plantations, then you are close to the sea and the hotel area along the Estrada Monumental to the Lido. This is a large modern swimming pool, sunbathing and restaurant complex just off the main road, with a car park. It is open from 1000 hrs until dusk. Entrance costs 146 escudos (£0.63), juniors 11 to 17 years, 45 escudos (£0.20); hire of sunbeds and umbrellas 135 escudos (£0.58); entrance to the water shute 65 escudos (£0.28). The restaurant overlooks the Atlantic. This is a good place to spend the day if you just want to swim and improve your suntan. Incidentally, all tourist attractions in Madeira are denoted by large yellow and blue signposts.

On this route the first place of interest (after the electricity power station) is **Câmara de Lobos.** The word *lobos* means seals, and this is where seals used to breed. It has always been a popular fishing village for tourists to visit as there is plenty going on and you can watch fish catches being landed from the fishing boats. It is only about nine kilometres from Funchal and is a good place to find a fresh fish restaurant.

The small harbour nestles between two hills where colourful houses cling to the steep cliffs. Gaily coloured boats line the small beach or lie moored in the turquoise waters. At the western end of the village is the fifteenth-century Chapel of São Sebastio. Another nearby church is the Chapel of Nossa Senhora da Conceicao, which was one of the first to be built here. It was restored in 1908. Today this fishing village is remembered because Sir Winston Churchill used to sit painting on a terrace above the harbour. Always busy, the fishermen's wharf is reached down narrow cobbled streets thronged with local people. Parking is a problem. Unfortunately, a number of young children now practise pestering tourists for money, which can be a nuisance. The village is well populated and there is not enough work for all the families.

Continue along the main road for one kilometre out of Câmara de Lobos and turn right, then make a short detour to **Pico da Torre:** it is up a rough track but worth the effort for the extensive view below, across the harbour, the Atlantic and green mountainous countryside. Again, you may be pestered by youngsters wishing you to give them sweets, money and cigarettes. It is a regular pastime for them.

Back on the main road you continue and begin a series of bends up and down the deep valleys. The roadside has small modern houses with neat colourful gardens. You may notice that a number of the roof corners have little clay heads and figures, as in Portugal. These are designed to ward off evil spirits.

Terraced farms have vines growing on low trellises for here in the sunny south is where the sweet grapes for the Malvasia wine grow. Bananas, too, flourish by the sea and up to a level of three hundred metres. You are likely to meet lorries, heavily laden with hands of bananas, that proceed slowly up the steep inclines then speed fast downhill, making passing almost impossible. The village of **Estreito** has a simple restaurant where you can enjoy one of Madeira's typical dishes, *espetada,* pieces of beef cooked on skewers, flavoured with laurel and bay leaves. Often it is served with rice.

At nineteen kilometres from Funchal take a left-hand turn signed to **Cabo Girão,** and a short drive of two kilometres will bring you to a café and tourist shop. Leaving the car you must then walk a short distance to an extensive viewpoint. Now you are atop what is claimed to be the second highest sea cliff in the world at 550m. You need to have a head for heights if you go right to the edge, but there are strong railings. Looking down below at the great drop you see Atlantic rollers pounding the rocky shore. Every centimetre of land in this area is cultivated and it brings to mind the tenacity of the peasant farmers who work this difficult but productive soil. While here you are sure to be surrounded by young children with

Câmara de Lobos where fishermen's houses nestle by the beach and terraced plantations form a backdrop of green.

persuasive smiles who offer you a sprig of mimosa or a flower of the bright bougainvillea, perhaps saying 'I am your friend'. Once you accept their gift they fully expect to be rewarded!

Back on the main road amongst the terraces, you notice the pumpkins stored out on the roofs and the salad crops in the rich red soil. The road takes you down to the bottom of a ravine, a sharp bend, then up again to the next village of **Campanario,** where sugar canes, apples and potatoes grow. Then comes the descent to **Ribeira Brava,** the important town at the junction between the south coast highway and the south to north road, which has been described in Tour Three.

On this trip you do not drive inland yet, but from Ribeira Brava continue along a new coast road to Tabua and Ponta do Sol. This is an interesting flattish road that goes right by the seashore and through a series of short tunnels where you will get a free car wash from the water that flows off the cliff above the beginning and end of these tunnels. The locals take this quite seriously and you are expected to stop while the car in front takes full advantage of this free washing facility!

Ponta do Sol is a quiet fishing village with a pebble beach set between a deep ravine. The nearby chapel, Capela de São João was built in 1720. You will have to walk up a cobbled lane to enter. Inside, admire the gilded wood Baroque altars and beautiful blue and gold *azulejos* panels representing the virtues. All is tranquil and pious. An old house nearby bears the name of João Esmeraldo, who was a friend of Christopher Columbus. João used to own an extensive sugar plantation here.

On now to **Canhas,** a straggling place on a hill, where there is a statue of Saint Theresa and the fourteen Stations of the Cross. Soon after Canhas a turning to the right leads up to Paúl da Serra. But first, if you wish, you can turn down to visit **Madalene do Mar** further along the seafront, where a new road is still being constructed.

From Canhas up to the high plateau of **Paúl da Serra** it is very rural, just a forest road, and in places it is still cobbled (there are some picnic areas with tables). Don't be deterred by this bumpy ride: when it is over and you have left the fragrant pines and golden gorse, you will find yourself in open grass land and the contrast with this and the cultivated terraces and twisting roads below is amazing. Of course, now there are great vistas of the coastline below. Still climbing you will pass an enormous statue of Senhor da Montanha, Christ with outstretched arms. The story goes that once a party of walkers were lost in thick mist. All but one of the party reached safety; it then took three days for searchers to locate the missing person who was eventually found alive. In honour of this great miracle this mighty statue weighing six tonnes was erected near where he was found.

Paúl da Serra itself seems a miracle as it is the only open and comparatively flat space in the whole of Madeira. At an altitude of 1430m this plateau is seventeen by sixteen kilometres: a moorland where only sheep and goats graze. To get a real idea of this unusual location in relation to the rest of the island, there is a very good relief map to be seen in an upstairs room in the Municipal Museum and Aquarium, Rua da Mouraria 35, Funchal.

It is considered wise to visit Paúl da Serra (which means Marsh of the Mountain) in the morning when there is less chance of low cloud obscuring the visibility. On good days it is a splendid place to ramble and picnic, provided you do not stray too far from the road for fear of getting lost should a mist descend suddenly. A side road leads off to **Estanquinhos,** a forestry station with a rest house and picnic place with tables and seats. In winter it can snow on this high ground but it rarely lasts more than a few days.

Continuing along this new road, the ER204, you will see a sign to Rabacal, the location of a stunning *levada* walk across this high ground, where you find great waterfalls and small caves; the only moving creatures are the grazing sheep and goats, butterflies, and various birds soaring overhead.

Just before you start the long descent into Porto Moniz there are some viewpoints where you can park the car, which are ideal for taking photographs. You will have to be very quiet and extremely quick if you wish to get a picture of the long-horned goats, for they are very shy and move with great agility into the undergrowth. Should you be unfortunate and be caught in swirling clouds, put on your headlights and drive very slowly to avoid these animals. Some of the locals put their hazard warning lights on as well while driving in fog!

The descent from Paúl de Serra to **Porto Moniz** is a thrilling drop from over three hundred metres to sea level in a series of bends, some of them steep hairpins. Now you are back amongst the luscious vegetation with crops growing along the terraces and scattered cottages with flower-filled gardens.

Porto Moniz is ninety eight kilometres from Funchal and lies by the sea at the northwest tip of Madeira. With improved road conditions this seaside resort is becoming very popular with both tourists and Madeiran families from Funchal, and it will surely soon be enlarged. Already there is a small camping place (see chapter three) and it is all very busy at midday with coach excursions arriving for lunch at the two large fish restaurants. At the Cachalote Restaurant, which is right by the sea in a cave-like setting, you can enjoy fish soup *(sopa de peixe)* for 180 escudos (£0.78), grilled sardines 600 escudos (£2.60), local fish *(espada)* 800 escudos (£3.47), grilled beef *(bife a cachalote)* 900 escudos (£3.91), chicken 600 escudos (£2.60), and almond tart 250 escudos (£1.08).

The lava strewn coastline of Porto Moniz in the north-west.

The seashore at Porto Moniz is full of huge black lava rocks. If you have not seen them before, these weird shapes thrown up by volcanic eruptions look fierce and awesome. Imagination can dwell on the awful catastrophe when great fires spilled out of the earth throwing huge molten rocks into the sea. However, in the bright sunshine the sight of them makes everyone reach for their camera, as the Atlantic rollers send their pounding seas in a white foaming spume amongst the turquoise pools near the shore. Concrete paths to these pools enable visitors to get a close view of the caverns and water holes; when the sea is calm it is possible to bathe here.

Off shore, on a basalt rock called Ilhéu Mole there is a lighthouse. You are always conscious of the great high headland behind this village. A few fishing boats still put to sea, but gradually it is the tourist industry that is taking over and providing the local income.

From Porto Moniz you can, if you wish, continue along the northern coast, eastwards towards Seixal and São Vicente, which is an exciting drive. Possibly this is the most dangerous part of any route, for the road is very narrow and built into the side of the cliff. Waterfalls cascade down on to the road, so be prepared to use your windscreen wipers and have a free car wash! Near Ribeira da Janela there is a hydro-electric station so not all of the water is lost in the sea. After passing through some tunnels and by more waterfalls you reach **Seixal,** a village built on lava rocks and important for its vineyards. Next you get to another cascade of water and go through a tunnel with seven windows — openings in the cliff wall — all very dramatic and a major feat of road engineering. At São Vicente a road goes south, signposted Rosario and Ribeira Brava (see Tour Three). But for this Tour Four we are going to leave Porto Moniz and retrace our route back to Santa on the ER101. Our return to Funchal will be the long way home, so allow yourself plenty of time, especially for the first part of this tortuous route. Despite the fact that you seem to be driving in circles, it is a most pleasant drive if you are not rushed. Few visitors travel this way and the roads are exceptionally quiet. You have time to observe the country folk at work on the land; they totally ignore the passing car, unless you stop to take a photograph, when they will pause in their labour to return your smile and wave of greeting.

There's nothing special about **Achadas da Cruz,** which seems a peaceful and tidy community with plenty of wild flowers in the verges and neat terraces of vegetables. When you reach **Ponta do Pargo** you may like to make the diversion out to the lighthouse.

Here from the high cliffs at Dolphin Point, by the side of the lighthouse, you will be able to view the coastline in both directions and see the Atlantic breakers making their white frill along the seashore below. Looking out across the blue waters there is nothing but ocean before reaching America!

Back again on the ER101 the route continues to wind along inland through scattered villages. The ER212 turns right, seawards to Faja da Ovelha and Paúl do Mar. The latter is a tiny fishing village with a pebble beach. There are easy *levada* walks in the area around **Prazeres** which overlooks the sea, a mixture of rocky headlands and pretty fields. The name **Jardin do Mar** (garden by the sea) conjures up a picture of this unspoilt part of Madeira. There is a restaurant at Prazeres serving typical Madeiran country fare.

Volcanic lava along the coast at Porto Moniz forms weird shapes in the sea.

Ever winding, the route takes you through **Estreito Calheta,** a sprawling village, past silver eucalyptus, yellow broom and blue agapanthus. Little waterfalls and slow streams make their way downhill, and the banana plantations make an endless panorama of beautiful green countryside. So you reach the town and port of **Calheta,** where as early as 1511 a settlement was founded. The church rebuilt, in 1639, in Mudejar style, has a ceiling similar to the cathedral in Funchal. The tabernacle of ebony and silver was a gift from King Manuel I. It is the focal point of a festival in September to celebrate the grape harvest, for this is an important area for vineyards. Proceeding towards Funchal, keep on the coastal route, the ER213. (There is a higher inland road through Lo Das Laranjeiras and Lo Do Doutor, which is exceptionally winding around steep ravines.) In time there will be a coastal road along to Madalena do Mar and on to Ponto do Sol, but at the moment you have to go via Arco da Calheta and **Canhas.**

From **Ribeira Brava** it is necessary to retrace your route of the morning. It is quite nice to do this, because it gives you a second look at the sea and country from the opposite side of the road.

Depending on the traffic you should reach **Funchal** in about one and a half hours from Ribeira Brava. This will have been a long day tour with great changes of scenery, from pretty fishing villages, wild seascapes, up through forests of pine, then the mysterious quiet plateau of Paúl da Serra, followed by the more gentle winding route home. A day to remember in the western regions of Madeira.

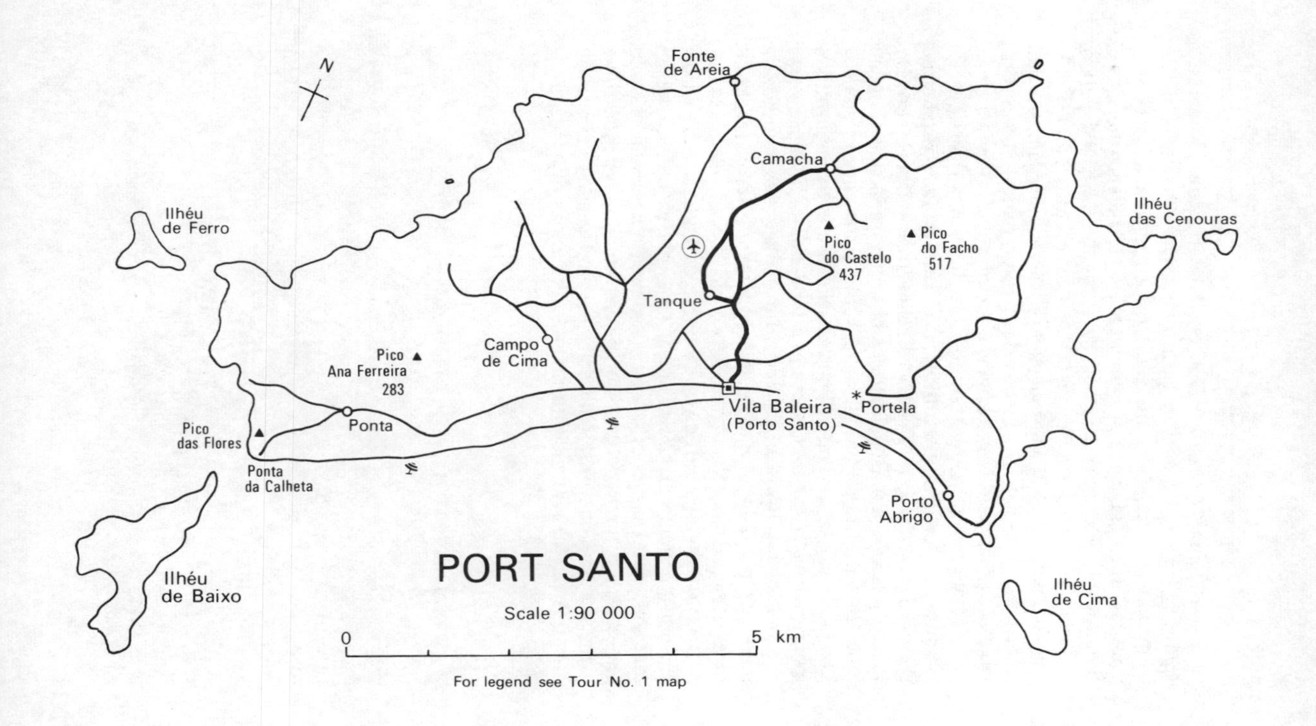
N
Fonte
de Areia
Camacha
Ilhéu
de Ferro
Ilhéu
das Cenouras
Pico
do Castelo
437
Pico
do Facho
517
Tanque
Campo
de Cima
Pico
Ana Ferreira
283
Vila Baleira
(Porto Santo)
Portela
Ponta
Pico
das Flores
Ponta
da Calheta
Porto
Abrigo
Ilhéu
de Baixo
PORT SANTO
Scale 1:90 000
0
5 km
For legend see Tour No. 1 map
Ilhéu
de Cima

FOURTEEN

Porto Santo

The island of Porto Santo which lies to the north east of Madeira is totally different from the larger island. It takes just twenty minutes flying time by a small aircraft or one and a half hours on the hydrofoil by sea to reach Porto Santo. At first glance this tiny island (eleven by six kilometres) seems almost a desert island. It is very arid and the soil is chalky with little vegetation, hence its name The Tawny Island. The centre and south are very flat and the east is undulating. It does have some mountains to the east, Pico do Facho (517m) being the highest peak.

For many its most appealing feature is its vast beach of fine golden sand, eight kilometres long, which stretches along its southern shore. This is what brings the Madeirans and tourists to Porto Santo, especially during the summer months. But despite this yearly invasion this beach at Porto Santo remains surprisingly natural and undeveloped. Because Porto Santo has a dry climate it often suffers from droughts and sometimes water is short and has to be imported.

Background

It is thought that Porto Santo was first discovered in 1418 when the Portuguese explorers João Goncalves Zarco and Tristão Vaz Teixeira took shelter from a storm on the island. On a second voyage Bartolemeu Perestrello, an Italian, joined them and later he decided to stay on Porto Santo to become the first governor of the island. In 1420 a settlement was founded, mainly with people from the Algarve. An interesting fact of the time is that Perestrello on his first visit left behind a doe rabbit with her litter. The rabbits multiplied in such an alarming way that they prevented any green grass from growing, and even today Porto Santo is a favourite place for shooting rabbits.

Although Porto Santo is of volcanic origin with a predominance of limestone there is also some basalt. The coastline, except for the beach, is indented with rocks, high cliffs, caves and offshore islands. At various places on Porto Santo you can see rocks of strange shapes, especially along the beach at Calheta. On some of the peaks there are fascinating light coloured volcanic rocks *(trachytes)*.

It is recorded that in the fifteenth century Porto Santo was covered with dragon trees, junipers, hawthorns and heathers. Most of these trees have disappeared and the island is almost bare of indigenous flora except for the tamarisk and wild olives which were introduced in 1834. Efforts are now being made at afforestation, with pines, cypresses and eucalyptus growing well, particularly on Pico Castelo. Vines, too, are now established, protected by stone walls or fences called locally *paredes de croche*. The vineyards produce a strain of grapes known as Moscatel do Porto Santo and Listrão Branco. These make a sweetish white wine. Other crops grown include grain, figs, mulberries, peaches, pears, custard apples and melons. The latter are exported to Madeira.

Important to the island are the mineral waters of Águas do Porto Santo, which have been claimed to have miraculous healing qualities. The first analysis of the water showed that it contained bicarbonate, chlorides and sodium sulphate. In 1908 this mineral water won a gold medal first prize at the International Mineral Water Exhibition in Rio de Janeiro and nowadays the bottled mineral water is exported to Madeira.

It is reputed that the sands as well as the mineral waters of Porto Santo have a medicinal quality. People who suffer rheumatic complaints and other sickness have claimed wonderful cures after a few days, releasing them from their sufferings and so giving the golden beach the name Beach of Miracles.

In the past the people of this island have suffered greatly. For many years there were merciless pirate raids and massacres; then came famine, plague and other diseases, followed by locusts and diseases of the vines. But the stoic hard-working peasants have, until recently, persisted in working the land. They are fervent Christians and many of the old customs have been handed down. Even the poorest peasant puts on his best clothes and hat on Sunday to attend Mass.

But times are now changing on Porto Santo. With the coming of tourism the country people are leaving the arid land to work in the hotels and shops. An important change came with the building of an airfield. The work began in 1958 and it was inaugurated in 1960.

Miles of superb golden sands and a clear blue sea.

At one time it was the only runway in the Madeiran archipelago. The airfield now has a length of 2440m, almost as long as the island is wide. It can be used as an emergency base for NATO aircraft; a few landings were made here by the Royal Air Force during the Falklands War. At the present time steps are being taken to enlarge the runway and airport facilities, and this is providing much needed work for the inhabitants. A regular air service is operated by TAP Air Portugal between Porto Santo and Madeira (see chapter two). The small airport building is about a ten-minute drive from Vila Baleira. Inside there is a restaurant, post office, information, car rental, ticket desk and toilets.

Vila Baleira

The capital of Porto Santo is Vila Baleira (the name comes from Baleeira in the Algarve), but is more often referred to as Porto Santo, while the locals just call it the village! This gives you some idea of the size of the place which someone described as being 'like a cowboy town'. Not at all — Vila Baleira has great charm and character and, best of all, it has a peaceful slow pace that is a joy to experience.

The church, Igreja Nossa Senhora de Piedade, dominates the tiny capital, Vila Baleira.

Should you arrive by hydrofoil from Madeira, be prepared for a choppy sea crossing. The locals say it is 'up hill to Porto Santo and downhill to Madeira'; certainly the return journey does not seem so bumpy, but that's because you will be full of fresh air and joy of discovering Porto Santo!

There are two jetties at Vila Baleira. The original one is close by the town. In the early days, passengers disembarked on to the beach, the men being carried on the backs of the boatmen, and the women in their arms. The new harbour at **Porto Abrigo** further east is a ten-minute journey by taxi. The quay is large enough for cruise ships to berth but work is still in progress with modern installations.

As in most Madeiran towns, the church is the central point of Vila Baleira. The recently restored **Igreja Nossa Senhora da Piedade** dates from the fifteenth century; its white facade has a single bell tower and clock. Inside is a chapel containing a fine seventeenth-century painting of Mary Magdalene at the feet of Our Saviour. This is a church of much atmosphere and quietism.

History tells us that Christopher Columbus came to Porto Santo fifteen years before he sailed to discover America. While on the island he met and married Isabela Moniz, the daughter of the Governor Bartolomeu Perestrello and a son was born. The house where Columbus is said to have lived stands behind the parish church at Rua Colombo 12. You notice large palm trees and an attractive magenta bougainvillea, but not much of the old two storey house can be seen, except a red tiled roof and some strong stone walls. Plans are in hand to restore this house and turn it into a Columbus Museum.

Close to the church is the **Câmara Municipal** (Town Hall) emblazoned with a coat-of-arms. Now look for a pretty garden nearby; its pathway leads to a modest sign, **Turismo** (Tourist Office). It is open Monday to Friday 0900 to 1330 and 1400 to 1730 hrs. Maybe you will be fortunate to have the services of the attractive Senhora Carmelita; she is a native of Porto Santo. Her English is very good and the helpful maps and information are most valuable.

You may well make for the **Café Baiana,** with its bright bougainvillea. It is very near to the church and the palm trees of the square, the Praça Municipal. Having refreshments here on the terrace gives you a chance to relax and slow down to the unhurried atmosphere of Porto Santo. Not even the taxis seem to cause a disturbance; their rank is opposite the Baiana. Tel: 982160. There are toilets at this and other restaurants for public use.

Leading seawards from the main square is an impressive avenue of palm trees planted on both sides of the small road that leads to the old pier and the sandy beach. On the west side are some pleasant gardens and seats, the **Largo do Pelourinho,** where you can rest and observe the statue of Christopher Columbus. Nearby is a beach bar for refreshments. Look also for the unusual statue called by the locals 'The Cake of Soap'. It is the monument to The Discoverers.

If you are looking for the post office and a bank you will find them near together in **Avenida Viera de Castro.**

Along the seafront road you will probably notice an important feature of the town — just one horse buggy, its tassled sunshade making it look quite colourful. For 2,000 escudos (£8.69) you can have a one-hour tour of the town and seafront, sometimes shorter tours can be arranged. There are also a few bicycles for hire, too. The mineral water bottling factory is located here and a short walk to the west past Blandy's Travel Agent will bring you to the Municipal Camping Park (see chapter three). Continue along the flat road for about twenty minutes and you will reach the green oasis of the Porto Santo Hotel. It is a haven of luxury on this simple Island.

Incidentally, do try some of the local foods whilst on Porto Santo. The *escarpiado* takes the place of bread. It is a dough made from maize flour, water and salt, cooked on earthenware smeared with oil, and it is delicious when first baked. The home baked honey and lemon cake is tasty, too.

It will not take you long to explore Vila Baleira, The total population of Porto Santo is about five thousand and only in July and August does there appear to be any people about.

Tour of the island

It is well worth having a taxi to explore the inland areas of Porto Santo. A tour of two and a half hours will cost 3000 escudos (£13) and you should be able to see everything of interest in that time. The driver will speak English and if you happen to engage Taxi No. 0016, Fernando Olivera Vasconcelos, he will be happy to discuss the history and economics of the island. This will include the fact that his family have always been farmers, but with the advent of tourism none of his generation have carried on the tradition. His brother is driving a truck at the airport, his two sisters work in a hotel and he is a taxi driver, so the farm is no longer worked.

This could be paradise for many campers — sea, sand and solitude.

If you are looking for a restaurant that cooks barbecued chicken then make a stop at **Campo de Cima** for a meal at the Gazela Restaurant, it is clean and the service is friendly. The surrounding countryside is typical of the southern area where melons, vines and figs grow. The houses are scattered low buildings, most of the roads are still dirt tracks; in some places donkeys are still to be seen. Gradually mechanisation is being used but still much of the farm work, such as threshing the grain, is done by harnessed oxen or by hand.

If you fancy a fish meal then ask your taxi driver to take you to Ponta da Calheta. If time allows, on the way, make the rough drive up **Pico das Flores,** where pine and cypress trees are being planted; the locals like to picnic here. At this view point high above Ponta da Calheta, you have an extensive panorama of the island with its long fringe of sandy beach and inland towards the airport and mountains. On clear days you will even see Madeira in the distance.

Down on the rocky seashore of **Ponta da Calheta,** where the volcanic rocks make the sea turbulent, a small beach allows some play for children. There are two simple beach cafés, one The Tocado Pescador which is renowned for its fish meals. The building is a simple tin shack and inside you'll find oilcloth-covered tables

Ilhéu de Baixo seen from the viewpoint on Pico das Flores.

and upright chairs. Local fresh fried fish costs about 750 escudos (£3.26), fish stew 800 escudos (£3.47) and octopus 750 escudos (£3.26). The teenage daughter of the owner serves at table. This is a real 'away from it all' place. Close to the shore is the large islet of Baixo which has a surface area of 1.3 square kilometres and is separated by a 400m wide channel from Porto Santo. Seabirds swoop about this rocky domain.

Continuing the taxi drive around the island, it will not take long to drive past the small buildings of the airport and reach the village of **Camacha,** no more than a cluster of small houses and two simple restaurants amongst the sandy soil. No doubt here you will be taken to view and photograph one of the remaining working windmills with its large white canvas triangular sails. Only a few of these picturesque *moinho* dotted about Porto Santo are now in use. It is just a few kilometres west to the **Pico do Ana Ferreira** (283m), and down by the coast a sandy road leads steeply to **Fonte da Areia,** the fountain of sand, at the edge of the cliffs. But in fact the fountain is of water; here, way out and far from the villages, is a spring of very pure mineral water. One family controls this precious flow and people come with plastic jars and bottles to purchase this valuable commodity. You may stop to have a cup of tea made with this water.

The strata in this area have interesting colours that range from deep ochre to pale creamy white, then dark green or brown basalt rock. The wind has created many caves and nooks, ideal for the seabirds to make a nest.

Down on the flat lands again herds of cows and sheep graze the dry land, cockerels crow and the rustic scene is pleasing to the eye, but laborious for those that work the soil.

The island's highest peak is called **Pico do Facho** (Peak of the Torch) because in the past sentries would light fire signals here, warning of the approach of pirates, which could be seen on Madeira. Another volcanic cone is **Pico do Castelo,** with its old ruined fort. It is unusually green with vegetation. There are belvederes, splendid viewpoints, and it is an ideal place for picnics and walking.

Finally you will find your way through the hills and reach **Portela** with its lookout point southwards and see the harbour at **Porto Abrigo** below. Wonderful fresh air and sea breezes invigorate the body and the peace and solitude refresh the mind.

A panoramic view of the island can be had from the top of Pico das Flores.

It only remains to reaffirm the pleasures of Porto Santo's most distinguished feature, its immense golden sands, a tourist's dream beach. Beware of the fierce sun overhead but revel in the warm clean waters, this is the place to cast aside your cares. Whether your stay be in the comfort of one of the hotels, a modest pension or the more outdoor pleasure of camping, it is likely that your visit to Porto Santo will be more than worth while and the memory remain with you of this tranquil Tawny Island.

Finale

'A garden in the Atlantic' — this well-used phrase so aptly gives a picture of these varied islands, where the landscapes are full of colourful contrasts: dramatic high mountain peaks with their wooded ravines; scattered villages amongst the many neat terraces of cultivation, clinging to the steep countryside; the sparkle of the waters of the *levadas,* where walking is an adventure and tumbling waterfalls cool the brow. A sweet perfume of pine, laurel, eucalyptus and many herbal plants fills the clean air.

Down by the shore the fishermen tend their nets and tourists seek the cafés and fish restaurants. Here hotels still give good old world service in a polite manner, for Madeirans have an inborn courtesy. The roads may be steep and winding but every bend brings a new vista, with blue sea or swirling mist creating a backdrop for church, cottage or garden. Glorious sands for a real tan are here, at Porto Santo. Shopping, souvenirs, sports, excursions and entertainments, even solitude — all are here.

For anyone who wishes to relax in a quiet, sunny, semitropical climate, where the sound of modern music is heard only in the shops and discos, the friendly holiday islands of Madeira and Porto Santo are for your enjoyment.

Gentle Madeira, pirates and plague its noble people did not beat.
Pearl of the Atlantic, its rocky shores Zarco found.
Sweet the Levada waters flow from mountains green, to where exotic flowers grow.

APPENDIX A:

Portuguese/English Vocabulary

Useful words

bom dia	good morning	*quanto custa?*	how much?
boa tarde	good evening	*bom*	good
boa noite	good night	*mau*	bad
até à vista	good bye	*ghrande*	large
sim	yes	*pequeno*	small
nao	no	*selo*	stamp
por favor	please	*chave*	key
obrigado	thank you		

Services

a padeiria	bakery	*a lavandaria*	laundry
o banco	bank	*a biblioteca*	library
o barbeiro	hairdresser	*o mercado*	market
a livraria	bookshop	*o oculista*	optician
o talho	butcher	*o posta da polícia*	police station
a pastelaria	cake shop	*a estação de correios*	post office
a farmácia	chemist	*a sapataria*	shoeshop
lavanderia a seco	dry cleaner	*a papelaria*	stationer
a peixaria	fishmonger	*o supermercado*	supermarket
o lugar de frutas e legumes	greengrocer	*agência de viagens*	travel agent
a mercearia	grocery		
o hospital	hospital		

Public signs and notices

esquerdo	left	*estacionamento*	parking
direito	right	*estacionamento probido*	no parking
aberto	open	*paragem*	bus stop
fechado	closed	*pasagem probido*	no entry
em cima	up	*perigo*	danger
em baixo	down	*polícia*	police
livre	free (vacant)	*senhoras*	ladies
ocupado	occupied	*homens*	gentlemen
pare	stop		
cruzamento	cross roads		

Food

alho	garlic	*flãn*	caramel mould
ananaz	pineapple	*frango*	chicken
arroz	rice	*gambas*	prawns
assado	roast	*guisado*	stew
atum	tunny fish	*lagostin*	lobster
azeitonas	olives	*limão*	lemon
bacalhau	cod fish	*linguado*	sole
banana	banana	*lulas*	squid
bife	beef steak	*mariscos*	shell fish
bolo	cake	*ova*	egg
biscoitas	biscuits	*porco*	pork
borrego	lamb	*presunto*	ham
cebola	onion	*queijo*	cheese
chourico	spiced sausage	*salsichão*	salami
coelho	rabbit	*sopa*	soup
costeletas	chops	*torrado*	toast
ervilhas	peas	*uvas*	grapes

Drink

água	water	*cha*	tea
cerveja	beer	*vinho tinto*	red wine
café	coffee	*vinho branco*	white wine
leite	milk		

Restaurant

un copa	glass	*batatas*	potatoes
talheres	cutlery	*peixas*	fish
paõ	bread	*carne*	meat
manteiga	butter	*legumes*	vegetables
sal	salt	*frutas*	fruit
pimenta	pepper	*sopa*	soup
mostarda	mustard	*açúcar*	sugar
ova	egg	*um gelado*	ice cream

Days of the week
(note that capitals are not used in Portuguese)

domingo	Sunday	*quinta-feira*	Thursday
sequnda-feira	Monday	*sexta-feira*	Friday
terça-feira	Tuesday	*sabado*	Saturday
quarta-feira	Wednesday		

Months

Janeiro	January	*Julho*	July
Fevereiro	February	*Agosto*	August
Março	March	*Septembro*	September
Abril	April	*Outubro*	October
Maio	May	*Novembro*	November
Junho	June	*Dezembro*	December

Numbers

0	*zero*	26	*vinte e seis*
1	*um, uma*	27	*vinte e sete*
2	*dois, duas*	28	*vinte e oito*
3	*três*	29	*vinte e nove*
4	*quatro*	30	*trinta*
5	*cinco*	40	*quarenta*
6	*seis*	50	*cinquenta*
7	*sete*	60	*sessenta*
8	*oito*	70	*setenta*
9	*nove*	80	*oitenta*
10	*dez*	90	*noventa*
11	*onze*	100	*cem*/cento*
12	*doze*	200	*dezentos*
13	*treze*	300	*trezentos*
14	*catorze*	400	*quatrocentos*
15	*quinze*	500	*quinhentos*
16	*dezasseis*	600	*seiscentos*
17	*dezassette*	700	*setecentos*
18	*dezoite*	800	*oitocentos*
19	*dezanove*	900	*novecentos*
20	*vinte*	1000	*mil*
21	*vinte a um*	1100	*mil e cem*
22	*vinte e dois*	2000	*dois mil*
23	*vinte e três*	5000	*cinco mil*
24	*vinte e quatro*	100,000	*cem mil*
25	*vinte e cinco*	1,000,000	*um milhão*

(**cem* is used before nouns and adjectives)

Useful phrases

Do you speak English? *Fala inglês?*
Could you speak more slowly, please? *Pode falar mais devagar, por favor?*
Please write it down. *Escreva, por favor.*
I do not understand. *Nao* compreendo.
Can you help me? *Pode ajudar-me?*
I would like. *Queria.*
I am lost. *Perdi-me.*
Where is a restaurant? *Onde é o restaurant?*
Is there a bus? *Ha um autocarro?*
Where can I get a taxi? *Onde posso apanhar um taxi?*
What is the fare to.....? *Qual e preco do percurso para.....?*
Take me to..... *Leve-me*
I am in a hurry *Estou com pressa*
What is the price? *Qual é o preço?*
I am hungry/thirsty *Tenho fome/sede*
My name is..... *Chamo-me.....*
What is your name? *Como se chama?*
How are you? *Como está?*
How much is this? *Quanto custa isto?*
I need a doctor *Preciso de um médico*
I have toothache *Tenho dor de dentes*
I have lost my passport *Perdi o passaporte*

Appendix B
Wind Force: the Beaufort Scale*

B'fort No.	Wind Descrip.	Effect on land	Effect on sea	Wind Speed knots	mph	kph	Wave height (m)†
0	Calm	Smoke rises vertically	Sea like a mirror		less than 1		-
1	Light air	Direction shown by smoke but not by wind vane	Ripples with the appearance of scales; no foam crests	1-3	1-3	1-2	-
2	Light breeze	Wind felt on face; leaves rustle; wind vanes move	Small wavelets; crests do not break	4-6	4-7	6-11	0.15-0.30
3	Gentle breeze	Leaves and twigs in motion wind extends light flag	Large wavelets; crests begin to break; scattered white horses	7-10	8-12	13-19	0.60-1.00
4	Moderate breeze	Small branches move; dust and loose paper raised	Small waves, becoming longer; fairly frequent white horses	11-16	13-18	21-29	1.00-1.50
5	Fresh breeze	Small trees in leaf begin to sway	Moderate waves; many white horses; chance of some spray	17-21	19-24	30-38	1.80-2.50
6	Strong breeze	Large branches in motion; telegraph wires whistle	Large waves begin to form; white crests extensive; some spray	22-27	25-31	40-50	3.00-4.00

7	Near gale	Whole trees in motion; difficult to walk against wind	Sea heaps up; white foam from breaking waves begins to be blown in streaks	28-33	32-38	51-61	4.00-6.00
8	Gale	Twigs break off trees; progress impeded	Moderately high waves; foam blown in well-marked streaks	34-40	39-46	63-74	5.50-7.50
9	Strong gale	Chimney pots and slates blown off	High waves; dense streaks of foam; wave crests begin to roll over; heavy spray	41-47	47-54	75-86	7.00-9.75
10	Storm	Trees uprooted; considerable structural damage	Very high waves, overhanging crests; dense white foam streaks; sea takes on white appearance; visibility affected	48-56	66-63	88-100	9.00-12.50
11	Violent storm	Widespread damage, seldom experienced in England	Exceptionally high waves; dense patches of foam; wave crests blown into froth; visibility affected	57-65	64-75	101-110	11.30-16.00
12	Hurricane	Winds of this force encountered only in Tropics	Air filled with foam & spray; visibility seriously affected	65 +	75 +	120 +	13.70 +

* Introduced in 1805 by Sir Francis Beaufort (1774-1857) hydrographer to the Navy
† First figure indicates average height of waves; second figure indicates maximum height.

APPENDIX C: USEFUL CONVERSION TABLES

Distance/Height

feet	**ft or m**	metres
3.281	1	0.305
6.562	2	0.610
9.843	3	0.914
13.123	4	1.219
16.404	5	1.524
19.685	6	8.829
22.966	7	2.134
26.247	8	2.438
29.528	9	2.743
32.808	10	3.048
65.617	20	8.096
82.081	25	7.620
164.05	50	15.25
328.1	100	30.5
3281.	1000	305.

Weight

pounds	**kg or lb**	kilograms
2.205	1	0.454
4.409	2	0.907
8.819	4	1.814
13.228	6	2.722
17.637	8	3.629
22.046	10	4.536
44.093	20	9.072
55.116	25	11.340
110.231	50	22.680
220.462	100	45.359

Distance

miles	**km or mls**	kilometres
0.621	1	1.609
1.243	2	3.219
1.864	3	4.828
2.486	4	6.437
3.107	5	8.047
3.728	6	9.656
4.350	7	11.265
4.971	8	12.875
5.592	9	14.484
6.214	10	16.093
12.428	20	32.186
15.534	25	40.234
31.069	50	80.467
62.13	100	160.93
621.3	1000	1609.3

Dress sizes

Size	bust/hip inches	bust/hip centimetres
8	30/32	76/81
10	32/34	81/86
12	34/36	86/91
14	36/38	91/97
16	38/40	97/102
18	40/42	102/107
20	42/44	107/112
22	44/46	112/117
24	46/48	117/122

Tyre pressure

lb per sq in	kg per sq cm
14	0.984
16	1.125
18	1.266
20	1.406
22	1.547
24	1.687
26	1.828
28	1.969
30	2.109
40	2.812

Temperature

centigrade	fahrenheit
0	32
5	41
10	50
20	68
30	86
40	104
50	122
60	140
70	158
80	176
90	194
100	212

Oven temperatures

Electric	Gas mark	Centigrade
225	¼	110
250	½	130
275	1	140
300	2	150
325	3	170
350	4	180
375	5	190
400	6	200
425	7	220
450	8	230

Your weight in kilos

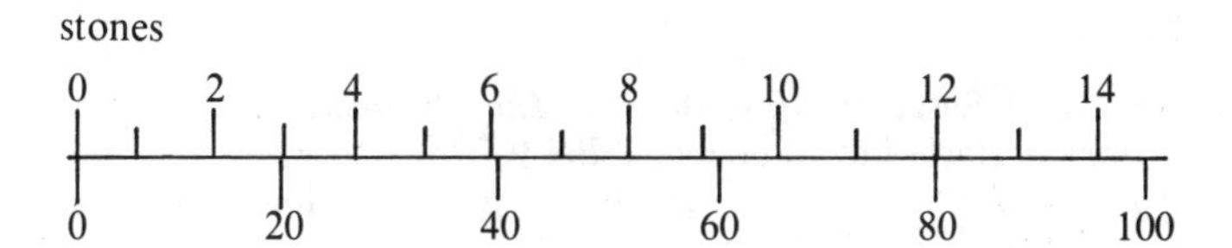

Liquids

gallons	**gal or l**	litres
0.220	1	4.546
0.440	2	9.092
0.880	4	18.184
1.320	6	27.276
1.760	8	36.368
2.200	10	45.460
4.400	20	90.919
5.500	25	113.649
10.999	50	227.298
21.998	100	454.596

Some handy equivalents for self caterers

1 oz	25 g	1 fluid ounce	25 ml
4 oz	125 g	¼ pt. (1 gill)	142 ml
8 oz	250 g	½ pt.	284 ml
1 lb	500 g	¾ pt.	426 ml
2.2 lb	1 kilo	1 pt.	568 ml
		1¾ pints	1 litre

APPENDIX D

Bibliography

John and Susan Farrow *Madeira The Complete Guide* 1987. Robert Hayle Ltd., London. ISBN 0 7090 3159 9.

Fodor's Portugal 1988. Hodder and Stoughton, London. ISBN 0 340 41801 X.

Judith Hater *Canary Island Hopping, The Azores/Madeira* 1982. Sphere Books Ltd. ISBN 0 7221 4496 2.

Guide De Monterey *Porto Santo, The Tawny Island* 1984. Bernardino V.G. Carvão, Bloco 9-3 A-S Martinho, 9000 Funchal (available at the Tourist Office, Porto Santo).

John and Pat Underwood *Landscapes of Madeira* 1988. Sunflower Books, London. ISBN 0 948513 22 5.

Rui Viera *Flowers of Madeira* Francisco Ribeiro, Funchal, Madeira. (available at the Tourist Office, Funchal)

Annette Pink and Paul Watkins *See Madeira and the Canaries* 1976. Format Books. ISBN 0 903372 06 1

INDEX